Guide to
Astrology

BROCKHAMPTON PRESS
LONDON

This edition published 1996 by Brockhampton Press, a member of
Hodder Headline PLC Group

ISBN 1 86019 316 1

Printed and bound in India

Contents

History

Astrology is an ancient craft that has its origin in the mists of time. It is impossible to place accurately the beginnings, but one thing that is certain is that astrology began as a subject intimately combined with astronomy. Its history is therefore the history of astronomy until the two subjects parted company, a split that essentially began when Nicolai Copernicus (1473–1543) published his book *De revolutionibus*. In this book he postulated that, contrary to earlier thinking in which the Earth was the centre of the solar system, the Sun actually formed the focus about which all the planets orbited.

It is thought that there was some study of these subjects five to six thousand years ago when Chaldean priests made maps of the skies. The Chaldeans were the most ancient of the Babylonian peoples. It was believed that heavenly bodies exerted influence upon man and whatever could not be ascribed to man must be due to actions of the gods or the deities of the planets. Subsequent study of the solar system began as pure observation because records and other data for calculation simply did not exist. The Egyptian and Greek civilizations gave much to the theories and practice of astrology, although much remained unwritten. It is said that the Chaldeans instructed the priests of the Pharaohs in astrology, and monuments exist that show a working knowledge of the subject. This was around 400–350 BC. A little earlier, in Greece around the beginning of the sixth century BC, the philosopher Thales (c.643–c.546 BC) studied astronomy/astrology as did Pythagoras (569–470 BC) who was credited by Copernicus as the person who developed the theory that the Earth and other planets revolved around the Sun.

There were many other Greek students, notably: Plato; Hippocrates, who combined astrology with medical diagnosis; Hipparchus, the founder of observational astronomy, who in 134 BC discovered a new star; and Claudius Ptolemaeus (100–178 AD). Ptolemy wrote the *Almagest*, which is a star catalogue of just over a thousand stars, and also a consideration of the motion of the Moon and the planets. He also wrote the *Tetrabiblos*, the earliest surviving book on astrology.

In Rome and the extended empire at this time, astrology was held in very high regard, and great faith was placed in the work and advice of astrologers who were appointed to the Emperors. The Moon was considered particularly influential and can be found depicted on many of their coins. Among the many Romans active in this field were Porphyry (232–304 AD), who is said to have developed the house method, and Julius Maternus (around 300 AD), who wrote a number of books on astrology.

From about 500 AD Arabs became the prime movers in science and philosophy, but by the early Middle Ages (the thirteenth century) interest was rekindled in Europe, at which time astrology had been divided into three distinct fields: *natural* or *mundane* astrology, which is prominent in forecasting national events, weather, etc; *horary* astrology, used to answer a question through the use of a chart drawn up for the actual time of asking; and *judicial* astrology, in which the fortune of an individual is determined by using a birth chart.

The fifteenth and sixteenth centuries in Europe saw the rise of several famous names, including the Polish astronomer Copernicus. Although Copernicus concurred with the views of Pythagoras, he could not prove the theory, and many attribute the real establishment of the principle (i.e. that the planets orbit the Sun) to Johannes Kepler (1571–1630), the German astronomer. The medieval precursor of chemistry was alchemy, and one famous practitioner was

Phillipus Aureolus Paracelsus (1493–1541), who also had some astrological leanings. He believed that the Sun, planets and stars influenced people, whether for good or evil. From this era also came Nostradamus (1503–1566). Michael Nostradamus has become one of the most famous of astrologists and prophets, and he also studied medicine. Almost from the outset it was thought that medical knowledge must, by necessity, include an understanding of astrology.

The work of the Dane Tycho Brahe (1546–1601) could, in some respects, be considered a watershed in the study of astrology/astronomy. Brahe became an observer of the heavens and in so doing was recognized as the most accurate since Hipparchus, centuries before. He prepared tables, designed instruments and studied the motion of the planets, particularly Mars, and it was this initial work that led Kepler to formulate his famous laws of planetary motion. Kepler was assistant to Brahe when the latter moved to Prague following the death of his patron, King Frederick. Kepler's work proved to be pivotal in advancing the understanding of astronomy. Kepler compared the work of Ptolemy, Copernicus and Tycho Brahe to produce three laws:

1. The orbit of each planet is an ellipse with the Sun at one of the foci (an ellipse has two foci.)

2. A line drawn from a planet to the Sun sweeps out equal areas in equal times.
3. The squares of the sidereal periods (time taken to orbit the Sun, measured relative to the stars) are proportional to the cubes of the mean distances from the Sun.

Kepler believed that the stars exerted an influence upon events and that astrology could predict the most mundane of happenings. During the sixteenth and seventeenth centuries there were many famous names who combined astrology with astronomy, mathematics or, commonly, medicine. These included the Italian physicist Galileo Galilei, a French professor of mathematics and doctor of medicine, Jean Morin, an Italian monk and mathematician, Placidus de Tito, and in England, William Lilly, who became famous as a practitioner of horary astrology and accurately predicted the Great Fire of London in 1666.

The poet John Dryden used astrology in predicting numerous events in his own life and the lives of his sons, including both their deaths. Following Dryden's own death in 1700, although not because of it, astrological practice declined on the continent but flourished in England. This influence extended to France at the start of the nineteenth century, where a sound scientific basis to the subject was sought.

William Allan (1800–1917), otherwise known as Alan Leo, was considered by many to be the father of modern astrology. He lectured widely throughout England and edited a magazine called *Modern Astrology*. He was also a professional astrologer and a prolific author on the subject, writing 30 books. In 1915 he founded the Astrological Lodge of London. Although the war years were disruptive to the study and practice of astrology, a large following was developed in North America. However, continental Europe suffered during the Second World War as Hitler's forces caused wholesale destruction, and Hitler himself, unhappy with adverse astrological predictions, destroyed books and records and incarcerated unfortunate practitioners.

Today astrology holds interest for many people, and growing numbers are becoming fascinated by its study. However, there is a dichotomy between astrology and astronomy.

The Solar System

The early visualizations of the heavens and the stars showed the Earth at the centre of a large revolving sphere. It was thought that the stars seen in the sky were somehow fastened onto the inner surface of this sphere. The stars that appeared to revolve around the Earth but did not move in relation to each other were called the 'fixed stars'. Among the many fixed stars there are some in particular that have certain characteristics and that can be used in astrological charts. For example, Regulus (or Alpha Leonis) is the brightest star in the constellation of Leo and signifies pride, good luck and success.

From early times it was noted that while many stars remained fixed, five in particular did not, and these wandered about the sky. These were the planets of the solar system because at that time not all eight remaining planets (other than Earth) had been identified. The discovery of Uranus, Neptune and Pluto followed the invention of the telescope, and Uranus was the first planet so observed, in 1781.

For the purposes of astrology, the Sun, which is actually a star, is considered as a planet. It is approximately 150 million kilometres from Earth and has a diameter of 1.4 million kilometres. Energy is generated in the core, from nuclear fusion, where the temperature is about fifteen million degrees.

The Planets

The Moon is a satellite of Earth but for convenience is also treated as a planet. It orbits the Earth roughly every 27 days, and the same face is always kept towards Earth, lit by light reflected from the Sun. The Moon seems to change size—the process known as waxing and waning—and it is called 'new' when it is situated between the Earth and the Sun and, because it is not illuminated, cannot be seen. The full Moon occurs about 14 days later, when the full face is totally illuminated.

Planets with their orbits between the Sun and the Earth's orbit are called 'inferior'. There are two planets in this category, Mercury and Venus. Mercury is the smallest planet in the solar system and takes 88 Earth days to complete one orbit, rotating slowly on its axis, and taking 58 Earth days for one revolution. Its elliptical orbit is eccentric, varying in distance from the Sun from 47 to 70 million kilometres.

Venus is the brightest planet seen from Earth and is

known as the morning or evening star. It is about 108 million kilometres from the Sun and has a diameter similar to Earth's, at 12,300 kilometres. Venus spins very slowly on its axis, and a day is equivalent to 24.3 Earth days, and a year is 225 days. It is unusual in being the only planet to revolve in the opposite direction to the path of its orbit.

The remaining planets, from Mars to Pluto, are called the 'superior planets', being on the distant side of Earth from the Sun. Mars takes about 687 Earth days to complete an orbit, and a day is just a fraction longer than one Earth day. The surface is solid and mainly red in colour because of the type of rock. There are many surface features, some of which are attributed to the action of water, although none is found there now. Mars is sometimes a dominant feature of the night sky, particularly when it occasionally approaches nearer to Earth, and it has from ancient times exerted considerable fascination.

Jupiter is the largest and heaviest planet in the solar system and has a diameter of 142,800 kilometres. The planet gives out more energy than it receives from the Sun and must therefore have an internal energy source. It is due, in part, to this that the atmosphere is seen to be in steady movement. Parallel bands of colour are seen, but a particularly noticeable feature is the Great Red Spot, which is thought to be an enormous storm, larger than Earth, coloured red because of the presence of phosphorus. The magnetic field of Jupiter is thousands of times stronger than Earth's, and radio waves emanate from the planet. Jupiter has 18 satellites, or moons, of which four are called the 'Galilean satellites'—Io, Europa, Ganymede and Callisto—because they were first seen by Galileo in 1610. There are three other groups of satellites, of which the innermost contains Adastrea, Amalthea, Metis and Thebe.

The next planet out from the Sun is Saturn, the second largest in the solar system. It has a diameter of 120,800 kilometres and the orbit takes 29 Earth years at a distance of 1507 million kilometres from the Sun. Because of its rapid rotation, Saturn is flattened at the poles with a consequent bulging at its equator. A day lasts for a little over 10 hours, and the surface temperature is –170 degrees Celsius. The most obvious and interesting feature of Saturn is its rings, which consist of ice, dust and rock debris, and some of which may have derived from the break-up of a satellite. The rings are about a quarter of a million kilometres across, and there are three main ones but hundreds of smaller ones.

Saturn also has 24 satellites, or moons, of which Titan is the largest with a diameter of 5200 kilometres (larger than Mercury). Some moons were discov-

ered by the Voyager spacecraft in 1989, including Atlas, Calypso and Prometheus.

The planets Mercury through to Saturn were all
known to astrologers and astronomers for many
years. The remaining planets, Uranus, Neptune and
Pluto, were discovered only in modern times, after
the advent of the telescope. These are therefore often
called the 'modern planets' by astrologers.

Uranus is 50,080 kilometres in diameter and a day
lasts 17 hours while a year is equivalent to 84 Earth
years. Because of its tilted axis, some parts of the
planet's surface are in light for about 40 years and
then in darkness for the remainder of its year. Uranus
was discovered by William Herschel in 1781 but was
something of a mystery until 1986 and the approach
of Voyager. It has a faint ring system and 15 moons,
some of which are very small indeed (less than 50
kilometres in diameter).

Neptune was discovered in 1846, but its existence
was earlier correctly postulated because of observed
irregularities in the orbit of Uranus. It takes 165 Earth
years to complete an orbit and is almost 4.5 billion
kilometres from the Sun. It is 17 times the mass of
Earth and has a diameter at its equator of 48,600 kilometres. There are three rings and eight known satellites, the largest of which, Titan, is similar in size to
the Earth's Moon.

Pluto, the smallest and most distant planet from the Sun, had its existence predicted because of its effect on the orbits of Neptune and Uranus and was finally discovered in 1930, although little is known about it. A day is equivalent to almost seven days on Earth, and a year is nearly 249 Earth years. Pluto has a very wide elliptical orbit, which brings it closest to the Sun (its *perihelion*) once in each orbit. Because of its great distance from the Sun (7.4 billion kilometres at its maximum), the surface temperature is very low, about 230 degrees. In 1979, one small moon, called Charon, was discovered, but since it is about one quarter the size of Pluto itself, the two act almost as a double planet system.

A Few Technicalities

As has been mentioned, the orbits of the planets are elliptical rather than circular, and there is a degree of eccentricity as well. When viewed from Earth, this combination of factors produces what may appear to be peculiar effects. For example, planets may move around the sky, slow and then appear to move backwards for a time. This apparent backward motion is called *retrograde motion* and is simply caused by the Earth moving more quickly through its orbit in comparison to another planet. It *seems* as though the planet being observed is moving backwards, but in reality it is moving forwards, albeit in the line of sight at a slower rate. It is similar to a fast train moving alongside a slow train, which makes the latter appear to be moving backwards. In astronomical tables *R* denotes retrograde while *D* marks a return to direct motion.

Another astronomical parameter used in astrology is that of conjunctions. A *conjunction* is when two or more planets (including the Sun of course) are in a line when viewed from Earth. On occasion, Earth, Venus and the Sun will all be in a straight line. If Venus is between Earth and the Sun it is called an 'inferior conjunction'. If, however, Venus is on the other side of the Sun from Earth, it is a 'superior conjunction'. The same applies to Mercury. *Opposition* is when, for example, Earth lies between the Sun and Mars; then Mars is in opposition. Opposition is when one of the superior planets (all except Mercury, Venus and, of course, Earth) is opposite the Sun in the sky, i.e. making an angle of 180 degrees when viewed from Earth. (*See* figure 1).

Of vital significance to the correct interpretive study of astrology are a number of parameters that enable the relative positions of planets to be fixed. These include the three great circles, one of which is the ecliptic, and the Zodiac. (A great circle is essentially any circle projected onto the celestial sphere whose plane passes through the centre of the Earth.) The horizon and celestial equator (the Earth's equator projected outward onto the celestial sphere) form two great circles, and the ecliptic is the third. The *ecliptic* is the path that the Sun apparently forms in the heavens. Of course the Earth orbits the Sun, but it seems from Earth to mark out a path that lies at an angle to the celestial equator. This means that the two lines cross twice, at the vernal and autumn equinoxes, oth-

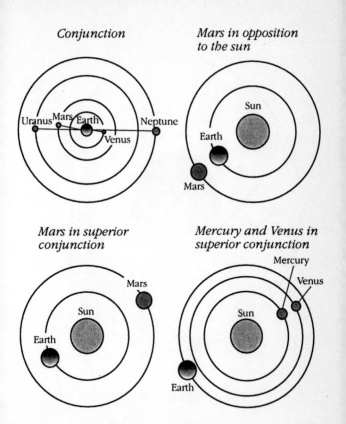

Figure 1: Conjunctions

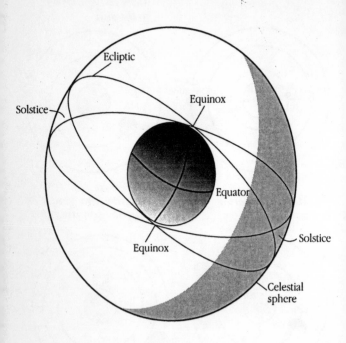

Figure 2: The ecliptic and the celestial sphere

erwise known as the March equinox (or first point of the sign Aries) and September equinox (or first point of the sign Libra). (*See* figure 2)

The two points at which the ecliptic is farthest from the celestial equator are called the solstices, and these occur in June for the summer solstice (when the Sun enters Cancer) and December for the winter solstice (on entering Capricorn). In the southern hemisphere these equinoxes and solstices mark the reverse situation.

The ecliptic itself is divided into twelve equal divisions, each of 30 degrees, one for each of the Zodiac signs. As the Sun apparently moves around the Earth, it goes from one sign of the Zodiac to the next. A person's Sun sign is the sign before which the Sun seems to be at the time of birth.

The *Zodiac* is a 'band' in the heavens that extends to seven or eight degrees on either side of the ecliptic. Within this band, or path, are contained the apparent movements of the planets, except Pluto. The solar system can be considered as a relatively planar feature, and within this plane the Earth revolves around the Sun. The planes of the orbits of all the other planets are within seven degrees of Earth's, save for Pluto, which is nearer 17 degrees. The Zodiac is then split into twelve segments of 30 degrees, one for each sign of the Zodiac and each represented by a particular star constellation (*see* figure 3). These signs are essentially a means of naming the sections of the sky within which the planets move. The constellation names, Scorpio, Libra, etc, have no significance although they are bound up in the development of the subject. It should be noted that today, the 30–degree segments no longer coincide with the constellation because of a phenomenon called *precession of the equinoxes*. Precession results in the Earth's axis of rotation not remaining in the same position but forming a cone shape traced out in space. It is due to the gravitational pulls of the Sun and Moon producing a turning force, or torque. This occurs only because the Earth bulges at the equator—a perfect sphere would not be affected. The Earth takes almost 26,000 years (known as the Great Year) to sweep out the cone, and in astrology the point Aries 0 degrees (the First Point of Aries), where the celestial equator cuts the ecliptic, moves with time. Because of precession, the equator crossing-point moves around the ecliptic, and now the First Point of Aries (the vernal equinox of astronomy) lies in the constellation of Pisces and is soon to move into Aquarius. The 30 degrees along the ecliptic that is Aries remains the 30 degrees counted from the vernal equinox, although that equinox is farther back each year (this is, therefore, retrograde motion). Aries has been considered the first sign from

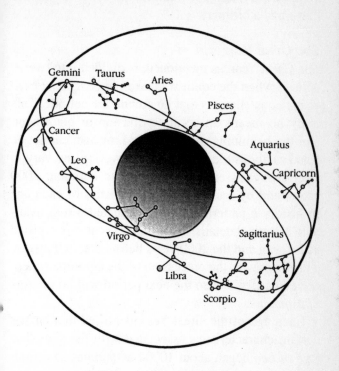

Figure 3: The Constellations

hundreds of years BC, when it was believed that the Earth had a birthday.

The Great Year

The Great Year, as mentioned, is divided into twelve periods when the equinox is taken to be against each of the constellations that lie around the ecliptic. This is by no means an accurate division or placement, and the beginning of each period, or age, cannot be fixed easily as the constellations overlap and vary in size. However, each age is taken to be about 2000 years, and by tracing the characteristics of each age in history a pattern can be constructed. From available historical details, the last 2000 years are typified as Piscean and the 2000 years before that as Taurean. This links with the precession of the equinoxes mentioned earlier, and so the next period will be the *Age of Aquarius*.

Each age of the Great Year identified this far has certain characteristics associated with the sign. The *Age of Leo* began about 10000 BC and has as its animal representative the lion, with which are connected creativity and regality. The Sun is its planet. It is interesting to note the early attempts at art, by way of prehistoric cave paintings, and of course the vital importance of the Sun in those times.

The *Age of Cancer* (8000–6000 BC) is associated

with the traits of home and family. At this time human beings began building dwellings, and some carvings symbolizing fertility have been found from this period.

From 6000 to 4000 BC was the *Age of Gemini*, which represents a sign of intellectual capacity. It is thought that writing began in some form during this Age, hence communication, a further characteristic of Gemini, became important. Civilization developed apace with cuneiform writing by the end of the Age, and the distinct possibility that human beings had begun to travel and explore.

The *Age of Taurus* followed, from 4000 to 2000 BC, and there are numerous instances that relate to the Taurean features of solidity and security with beauty. These traits are seen in the Egyptian dynasties and the worship of the bull, and in the enormous and ornate temples and the pyramids.

The next age is that of *Aries* (2000 BC–0 AD). Aggressive and assertive qualities are associated with Aries, as are physical fitness and supremacy. These are balanced by courage and also harmony. All these characteristics are well exemplified by the Greeks, who dominated in battle and architecture and yet created the first democratic government. The symbol of the ram found an outlet in numerous ways, including as an emblem of the Roman army.

We are currently in the *Age of Pisces* (0–2000 AD), albeit towards the end of the period. It began with the birth of Christ, and there are numerous connections to the sign of the fish at this time. The secret symbol for the early Christians was the fish, Jesus was called *Ichthus*, the fish, and many of his disciples were fishermen. Qualities such as kindness, charity and forgiveness are typical, as is selflessness, although an element of confusion can also be discerned. We are on the brink of the new Age, that of *Aquarius* (2000–4000 AD), but in many respects the signs are already there to be seen. Aquarian influence can be seen in the strong presence of science and technology and space travel. Also Aquarian is a sense of detachment and of being impersonal.

Signs and Symbols

Each sign of the Zodiac has a particular graphical representation, called a glyph, which itself relates to an animal or something similar. The same applies to the planets, and these symbols are used extensively, with others, in constructing an astrological chart. The Zodiac sign and symbols are as follows:

Aries
Representation: the ram's horns
Name: The Ram

Taurus
Representation: the bull's head
Name: The Bull

Gemini
Representation: two children
Name: The Twins

Cancer
Representation: breasts
Name: The Crab

Leo
Representation: the heart, or the
lion's tail
Name: The Lion

Virgo
Representation: the female genitalia
Name: The Virgin

Libra
Representation: a pair of scales
Name: The Balance

Scorpio
Representation: the male genitalia
Name: The Scorpion

Sagittarius
Representation: the Centaur's arrow
Name: The Archer

Capricorn
Representation: a goat's head and fish's tail
Name: The Goat

Aquarius
Representation: waves of water or air
Name: The Water-bearer

Pisces
Representation: two fish
Name: The Fishes

The glyphs of the planets are as follows:

 Sun

 Moon

Mercury

Venus

Mars

Jupiter

Saturn

Uranus

Neptune

Pluto

These planetary symbols are all made up of essentially the same elements, the cross, the half-circle, and the circle, all in different combinations. These pictorial representations are linked with the very early days of human beings, when communication was achieved using such graphical methods. As such, these elements each have a particular significance:

—the circle represents eternity, something without end, the spirit;
—a circle with a dot inside signifies that the spirit or power is beginning to come out;
—the cross represents the material world;
—and the semicircle stands for the soul.

The Signs of the Zodiac

The signs appear to have got their names from the depths of history and prehistory, and do not necessarily concur with their astronomical counterparts, the constellations. In some civilizations, the signs were attributed to parts of the body. The likeliest race to have adopted this were the Greeks, who also linked the signs to various plants.

Aries	–	the head
Libra	–	the kidneys
Taurus	–	the throat
Scorpio	–	genitalia
Gemini	–	hands and arms
Sagittarius	–	hips and thighs
Cancer	–	the breasts
Capricorn	–	the knee
Leo	–	the heart
Aquarius	–	calf and ankle
Virgo	–	the intestines
Pisces	–	the feet

Below are given the main features of the signs of the Zodiac, and these will be followed later by a fuller description of the character and personal details associated with the various sun signs, i.e. when the Sun passes through each of the signs as it appears to move on the ecliptic.

Aries

The astrological new year occurs around 21 March, when the Sun enters Aries, and this new aspect is mirrored in typical Arian traits of energy, keenness and enthusiasm. The Arian can be something of a pioneer and thus somewhat self-centred with a selfish streak. Aries is the most personal of the signs.

Taurus

Taureans seek and reflect stability, security, and are generally practical with a possessive side to their character. Risks will be taken only if they are absolutely essential, and even then it will be only after a great deal of careful thought. In general Taureans are trustworthy and pleasant and yet unenterprising, which in some may lead to them become a little boring.

Gemini

This third sign of the Zodiac is that of the heavenly

twins, which, not surprisingly, can surface as a certain duality, which in a negative sense may result in
someone being two-faced. Geminians are intelligent,
quick of mind, versatile, and are often good communicators. If the dual nature is too strongly negative
then it may lead to a lack of achievement through being over-committed and trying to do too many things
at once.

Cancer

Changeable, sympathetic, kind, hard on the outside
but easily hurt or offended, emotional and devoted—
a home and family builder. These are all Cancerian
traits and paint an essentially sensitive picture but
with the strengths of devotion and faithfulness. Intellectually, Cancerians are very intuitive and have a
strong imagination. If these traits are over-stressed or
misused, it can lead to restlessness and over-worry.

Leo

Leo is the only sign ruled by the Sun and, like the
lion, so-called king of the beasts, the Leonian can be
regal, dignified and magnanimous. They are faithful,
trusting but strong-willed, with fixed principles and
ideas, and yet if carried too far this may result in
bossiness. Similarly, someone may become snobbish,
conceited and domineering.

Virgo

Virgoans are typically worker types; they dislike a leading role in anything, and yet they are intellectually very capable, although with a tendency to worry. In work and at home they pay attention to detail with precision and clarity. Closeness to others may be avoided, resulting in the perception among others of Virgoans keeping to themselves, which in turn may be misinterpreted as inhospitality.

Libra

This seventh sign of the Zodiac is opposite to Aries, which makes Librans interested in relating to a partner. As such they tend to be companionable, tactful and like to be in pleasant surroundings. Librans are often unfairly dubbed as lazy. They may also have a tendency to be quite aggressive. A Libran may be of the type who sits on the fence over an issue and, seeing both sides of an argument, may be impossibly indecisive.

Scorpio

This sign is one of intense energy, with deep, passionate feelings about the object of their attention, be it a person or an issue. Scorpions can be passionate, but in excess this can result in resentment, jealousy and even hatred. However, they can equally be warm

and charming, and their virtues become apparent
when dealing with real life rather than more trivial
matters.

Sagittarius

In the earlier days of astrology, Sagittarius was always represented by a man joined to a horse, signify-
ing the duality of the sign—a combination of strength
and intelligence. Sagittarians are often intellectuals
with a thirst for a challenge and an ability of body and
mind to match. Taken to extremes, these traits can
mean restlessness, carelessness, extravagance and a
tendency to 'horseplay'.

Capricorn

Capricornians tend to be practical, ambitious and caring, and they often possess an excellent sense of humour. In personal relationships caution is their
watchword but once decided they will make good
partners. Capricornians are also traditionalists and
excel in routine work or in organizational capacities.
On the negative side, they may become too mean and
stern, and caution may turn into selfishness.

Aquarius

Aquarians are typically independent and individualistic, and also friendly. Indeed, friendships once

formed tend to be faithful, although contact with others can be rather impersonal. The freedom required by an Aquarian makes them paradoxical when it comes to love. However, the enquiring mind and originality is seen to good effect in pursuit of art or working in science and technology. An excess of Aquarian traits produces someone who is rebellious, tactless and eccentric.

Pisces

The last sign of the Zodiac, Pisces, is typified by a sensitivity that may border on the inhibited unless encouraged. Pisceans can be inspired and highly intuitive, although this may be clouded by mood swings, from elation to depression. Kindness is a common trait, and there is often a strong spiritual faith. In excess, Piscean characteristics may result in muddled thinking, weakness of character and excessive worry.

Groups of the Zodiac and Rulings

The twelve signs of the Zodiac are traditionally subdivided into a number of groups. The members of each group share certain characteristics that in terms of chart interpretation provide additional information rather than primary details.

The first grouping is the *triplicities*, otherwise known as the elements, and consists of the signs for fire, earth, air and water. Aries, Leo and Sagittarius are the *fire triplicity*. This sign is represented by a keenness and enthusiasm and a tendency literally to burn with excitement. Often more sensitive people will be considered slow and dealt with impatiently. While people with the fire sign may be lively and exuberant, their fault will often be that they are too lively. However, such tendencies are likely to be offset, to some extent, by features elsewhere in a chart.

The *earth triplicity* contains Taurus, Virgo and Capricorn and, as might be expected, people with this sign are 'down to earth', although the earth sign is not

43

totally dominant. However, the beneficial aspects include practicality and caution, and although considered dull by livelier people, there is a reassuring solidity and trustworthiness about people with this sign.

Gemini, Libra and Aquarius form the *air triplicity*, and communication is one of the key attributes. An 'ideas person' would have this sign prominent in his or her chart, but a potential fault can be that schemes and ideas occupy too much time at the expense of productivity. In addition, such people can be dismissive of sensitivity or caution in others.

The final triplicity is that of *water*, and it contains Cancer, Scorpio and Pisces. Such people are naturally sensitive and intuitive, and often inspired, while also emotional and protective. Such people tend to be cautious of those with strong personalities, and their own faults may result from being too emotional.

It is often the case that people who have a shared strength in these signs will be compatible. Reference to the elements produces obvious attractions:

Fire   air fans the flames while water puts them out and earth smothers them.

Earth water refreshes it while air and fire dry it out.

Air   fire responds to air, while earth and water restrict it.

Water earth holds it, but air and fire diminish it.

The *quadruplicities* (otherwise known as qualities) form the second grouping. In this case the signs of the Zodiac are divided into three groups of four. The three qualities are 'cardinal', 'fixed' and 'mutable'. Aries, Libra, Cancer and Capricorn are of the *cardinal quadruplicity*. People with this sign dominant in their chart are outgoing and tend to lead. Taurus, Scorpio, Leo and Aquarius are of the *fixed quadruplicity*, which implies stability and a resistance to change. The *mutable quadruplicity* includes the remaining signs, Gemini, Sagittarius, Virgo and Pisces, and all have an adaptability. They often appear selfless.

The third grouping is into positive and negative (otherwise known as masculine and feminine). In essence these are descriptive rather than definitive terms and equate in a general sense to being self-expressive or extrovert (positive) on the one hand and receptive or introvert on the other. This does not mean that if a woman has a masculine sign she is not to be considered feminine, and vice versa.

Taking into account the three groupings, the Zodiac signs are as follows:

> Aries   –   fire, cardinal, masculine
> Taurus   –   earth, fixed, feminine
> Gemini   –   air, mutable, masculine

Cancer	–	water, cardinal, feminine
Leo	–	fire, fixed, masculine
Virgo	–	earth, mutable, feminine
Libra	–	air, cardinal, masculine
Scorpio	–	water, fixed, feminine
Sagittarius	–	fire, mutable, masculine
Capricorn	–	earth, cardinal, feminine
Aquarius	–	air, fixed, masculine
Pisces	–	water, mutable, feminine

When interpreting charts, another useful link between signs is *polarity*. This is the relationship between a sign and the opposite sign across the Zodiac. Thus, on a circular display of the twelve signs, Aries is opposite Libra, Cancer opposite Capricorn, Taurus opposite Scorpio, etc. The signs thus opposed do not, however, have opposite tendencies; rather, the polar signs complement each other.

Before turning to the concept of ruling planets, it will be helpful to consider a few other definitions and some lines and angles that are critical in the construction of a chart. The *ascendant* is defined as the degree of a sign (or the ecliptic) that is rising above the horizon at an individual's birth and marks the junction of the first sign. This is essentially the beginning for any astrological chart construction and interpretation, and after calculation is marked on the chart, working clockwise upwards from the horizon line, which runs east-west across the chart. The ascendant is very significant and can only be constructed if a birth time is known. The significance of the ascendant is that it indicates the beginning of the personality and how an individual faces the world—his or her true self. There are many other factors that may lessen the influence of the ascendant sign, but if some characteristic comes out of a chart that reinforces one linked to the ascendant, then it will be a very significant trait.

The *descendant* is the point opposite to the ascendant, at 180 degrees to it, and is always the cusp, or junction, of the seventh house. Although it may often be left out of charts, the descendant is meant to indicate the sort of partner, friends, etc, with whom one associates and feels comfortable.

The *midheaven* is often abbreviated to MC, from the Latin *medium coeli*. At the time when one particular sign of the Zodiac is appearing over the horizon (the ascendant) there will inevitably be another sign that is at its greatest height. This sign is then said to culminate at the upper meridian of the appropriate place—in brief, the midheaven is the intersection of the meridian (*see* figure 2) with the ecliptic at birth. The significance of the midheaven is that it relates to the career of an individual and the way in which it is pursued. It can also provide a general indication of aims and intentions and the type of partner that may be sought. The point opposite to the midheaven is the *imum coeli* and is connected to the subject's origins, his or her early and late life, and parental/domestic circumstances. The *imum coeli*, or IC, is sometimes referred to as the nadir, but strictly speaking this is incorrect. The nadir is actually a point in the heavens that is directly opposite the zenith, which itself is a point in the heavens directly over any place.

Influence of the planets

Every sign of the Zodiac has what is called a *ruling planet*, which is the planet that rules the ascendant sign. From the list below, it can be seen that if someone has Pisces rising, the ruling planet will be Neptune. Each planet rules one sign, save for Venus and Mercury, which each rule two. Of course, before William Herschel discovered Uranus in 1781 there were only seven planets (including the Sun and Moon) and therefore three further planets ruled two signs; Saturn ruled Aquarius in addition to Capricorn, Jupiter ruled Pisces in addition to Sagittarius, and Mars ruled Scorpio in addition to Aries.

There are also a number of planets that are termed personal. The *personal planets* are the Sun and Moon (which are always personal), the planet that rules the ascendant sign (called the chart ruler). The Sun ruler is the planet that rules the Sun sign, and the planet that rules the sign occupied by the Moon is called the Moon ruler.

These different rulings were established a long time ago. There are additional features and weightings given to the rulings, known as *exaltation, detriment* and *fall*. Each planet is exalted when it is in a particular sign from which it works well and with which there is a notable similarity, resulting in more significance being attributed to it in an interpretation. The exaltations are also listed below:

Planet	Sun
Ruling in	Leo
Exalted in	Aries
Detrimental	Aquarius
Fall	Libra
Planet	Moon
Ruling in	Cancer
Exalted in	Taurus
Detrimental	Capricorn
Fall	Scorpio
Planet	Mercury
Ruling in	Gemini and Virgo
Exalted in	Virgo
Detrimental	Sagittarius
Fall	Pisces

Planet	Venus
Ruling in	Taurus and Libra
Exalted in	Pisces
Detrimental	Aries
Fall	Virgo
Planet	Mars
Ruling in	Aries
Exalted in	Capricorn
Detrimental	Libra
Fall	Cancer
Planet	Jupiter
Ruling in	Sagittarius
Exalted in	Cancer
Detrimental	Gemini
Fall	Capricorn
Planet	Saturn
Ruling in	Capricorn
Exalted in	Libra
Detrimental	Cancer
Fall	Aries
Planet	Uranus
Ruling in	Aquarius
Exalted in	Scorpio
Detrimental	Leo
Fall	Taurus

Planet	Neptune
Ruling in	Pisces
Exalted in	Leo
Detrimental	Virgo
Fall	Aquarius

Planet	Pluto
Ruling in	Scorpio
Exalted in	Virgo
Detrimental	Taurus
Fall	Pisces

The ruling planets and relationships

Opposing the ruling sign of the Zodiac, each planet also has a sign of detriment, from which it works less well. In this the planet is said to be weak or debilitated. The signs of detriment are listed in the table above. Finally, in this section comes the sign opposite to exaltation, which is called the fall sign. This is the sign of the Zodiac directly opposite to the sign of exaltation and, as with detriment, is where the planet is thought not to work as well. (*See* list above).

The Houses of the Chart

The astrological chart is divided into houses—in effect this is a way of subdividing the space around the Earth. There are numerous such systems, which have been devised over the years and which fall into three groups: the Equal House System; the Quadrant System; and a variation on these systems.

The *Equal House System* (*see* figure 4) is one of the oldest and after a period of disuse is now back in favour. The ecliptic is divided into twelve equal parts, and the houses are marked by great circles that meet at the poles of the ecliptic and start by going through the degree of the ecliptic ascending over the horizon, and then through every point 30 degrees farther around.

The main *Quadrant Systems* are called after the people who developed them, for example, Campanus, Regromontanus and Placidus, and appeared in the thirteenth, fourteenth and fifteenth centuries respectively. The system of Placidus was used almost exclusively until the early 1950s because it was the only

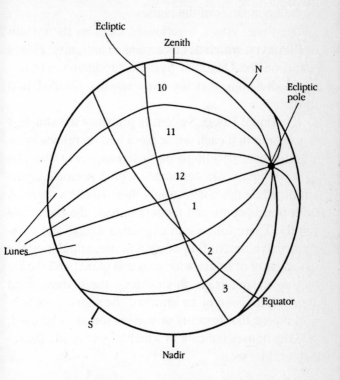

Figure 4: The Equal House System

system with published reference tables. It was, however, the only system that did not utilize great circles as the boundaries of the houses.

The final system, a variation, includes the system of Porphyry, which has its origins in antiquity. This is based on the Quadrant System, producing four unequal divisions that are then equally divided into three.

The Equal House System is probably the simplest to use, and in it each house has a certain relevance or significance, affecting a particular aspect of life. The first six houses are concerned with a personal application while the last six apply more to one's dealings with other people and matters outside the home and family. There follows an expanded though not comprehensive description of each house, stipulating the association of house with sign and planet and the resulting meanings. In this context, the planets stand for the provision of an impetus; the signs show how and where that impetus or motivation is to be used; and the houses indicate in which aspect of life the result will be seen.

The Houses

The First House
This house is associated with Aries and the planet

Mars, and because it includes the ascendant, or rising sign, is the most important house of the birth chart. This house refers to the person, which may include such factors as physical characteristics, nature, health, ego and so on. Planets within eight degrees of the ascendant will strongly affect all aspects of the person, including behaviour.

The Second House

The second house is associated with Taurus and the planet Venus, and is concerned with the possessions and feelings of the person. As such, this house reflects attitudes to money, and since money and love are intimately entwined, this aspect will be of relevance when interpreting a chart. The second house is also concerned with priorities and the growth of things.

The Third House

This is the house of Gemini and the planet Mercury, which not surprisingly means a concern for siblings and also neighbours. Other matters of a local nature, such as schooling, local travel and everyday matters of business, fall under this house. A combination of these factors with mental attitude, which also falls into the third house, means that many decisions and patterns of behaviour, of fundamental importance, can be considered here. Decisions such as where to live and personal environment are typical examples.

All aspects of communication also fall within this house, including speech, letters, teaching, and so on. For anyone who is lost as to which direction to go in or what decision to take, a positive influence from the third house will help him or her to adjust mentally and escape the impasse.

The Fourth House

The sign of Cancer and the Moon are associated with the fourth house. The key concerns of this house are the home itself, home circumstances and the family, and caring for someone or something. The mother, or a mother figure, is a particularly strong feature of this house. The concept of the home and the protective enclosing also has analogy with the womb and the grave—thus, the beginning and end of life are also concerns.

The Fifth House

This house is very different from the fourth, and the association of Leo and the Sun makes it the house of pleasure and creativity. This includes all such aspects, whether they be related to art, authors, games, gambling, and other leisure pursuits. Moving into the more personal sphere, the fifth house also accounts for lovers and love affairs, probably on a superficial level rather than a lasting, deep relationship. The other personal manifestation of creativity, that of producing children, and parents' feelings about children and procreation, fall under the rule of this house.

The Sixth House
The sixth house is the last that impinges upon the person and personal acts, behaviour and relationships. Its sign is Virgo and the planet is Mercury. This is a very functional house, referring as it does to work of a routine nature, health and similar matters. The work may be in the work place, hence it also relates to employers, or at home in the daily round of chores. The concern of health also includes diet, and this house will help to assess the need and timing for a change.

The Seventh House
The last six houses refer to the wider influences of one's life and to outward rather than inward application. Libra and the planet Venus are associated with the seventh house, and the fundamental concern is with relationships with others and partnerships. This house concerns commitment in partnership and can reflect the likely type of partner sought. It can also relate to the establishment of a business or the employment of new people, from the viewpoint of per-

sonal interaction. Because this house encompasses dealings with others, it can also include hostility and conflict.

The Eighth House

This house, the opposite of the second, is associated with Scorpio and Pluto, and refers to possessions gained through others, whether as gifts or legacies. In fact, all financial matters such as tax, joint money, insurance and corporate finances fall within this house. It is also the house of birth and death, or alternatively beginnings and endings. Deep relationships, including those of a sexual nature, are dealt with, as are matters of the occult, and those of the afterlife.

The Ninth House

The ninth house, the house of Sagittarius and Jupiter, is from the opposite of the third, which is concerned with neighbours and matters local. The ninth focuses upon travel and mental activity but on a widespread basis, i.e. it covers travel (to foreign countries) and extensive study (as is further education), and also has been called the house of dreams. Longer-distance communication and matters such as the law and literature are covered by the ninth house. Indeed, all factors that potentially may increase one's experience or awareness are appropriate.

The Tenth House
The fourth house is concerned very much with matters of the home and family—a seemingly introspective vision. The tenth house is its opposite and looks outward to life in general, being concerned with hopes and ambitions and making one's way in life. It used to be called the house of the carer and the father, when perspectives and opportunities were more limited than today. As such this is the province of the long-term carer and also denotes responsibility in the context of the delegation, both giving and receiving. This house is pertinent when career changes are considered, and is associated with Capricorn and Saturn.

The Eleventh House
The eleventh house is associated with Aquarius and Uranus. It is the house of acquaintances, social contacts and friends (but not close friends), and as such may encompass societies, clubs and similar groupings. It also provides an indication of whether a person looks favourably upon charitable causes and whether any activities in this direction are genuine or for the self—the house of social conscience in effect. It was called the house of hopes and wishes.

The Twelfth House
The twelfth house, associated with Pisces and Nep-

tune, is linked with things that are hidden, self-sacri-
fice, psychic matters and also matters of an institu-
tional nature. This last aspect may refer to hospitals
or prisons, and as such may include the more serious
illnesses. It can also shed light on problems of a psychological nature, reflected to some extent in its pre-
vious name—the house of sorrows.

As implied earlier, in The Signs of the Zodiac, the
following chapter on the Sun signs, or the Sun
through the signs, provides more information on personality, characteristics, associations and aspects of
personal involvement and interaction.

The Sun Signs

sign: **ARIES**
dates: 21 March to 20 April
origin and glyph: the ram's horns, which
  may be traced back to Egypt
ruling planet and groupings: Mars;
  masculine, cardinal and fire
typical traits: Arians have several noticeable characteristics, such as courage, seemingly boundless energy, enthusiasm, initiative and enterprise, and a desire for adventure and travel. This means that when
faced with a particular challenge, there is a tendency
to rush in without heeding the consequences, and
this can often cause problems. This impulsiveness
is, of course, one of their less appealing traits, and it
may also be accompanied by selfishness. This manifests itself in the need to accomplish set tasks and
reach planned goals, although they tend to have the
beneficial quality of being able to concentrate on the
primary aim by removing anything that is unneces-
sary and of little importance. Competitiveness is

never far from the surface for an Arian, no matter what aspect of life is involved.

en famille: in personal relationships, Arians can be very passionate, and Aries men look for a strong partner. Arian women are equally demanding and often prefer a career to being at home, although the two can be combined. Providing there are no adverse influences elsewhere on a person's chart, Arians are faithful but there are those who are continually moving on to new relationships and challenges.

Children of this sign tend to show the typical traits of liveliness and enthusiasm, but because there is always an underlying impatience, a child may soon lose interest and be looking for something new. Performance at school may be chequered because of this trait. However, should such a child lose his or her place or standing, his or her natural competitiveness and wish to lead usually reassert themselves, and lost ground is regained and held.

As parents Arians are, not unexpectedly, energetic and in the main will encourage their children in a variety of activities. It is all too easy, however, for the ebullience of the parent to overshadow the wishes of the child, and that can easily result in discord.

business: to satisfy the Arian character, an occupation ought to be challenging, with goals to aim for

and with the opportunity to lead. Boring, routine
jobs would not satisfy, but if that were the outcome
then other activities would have to compensate.
Large organizations with some freedom and a defined career structure, such as teaching, the police or
the civil service, would be appropriate.

wider aspects: in their other pursuits, Arians import
their eager approach, which in certain circumstances can be positively damaging, for example,
knocks and bruises in the early years.

associations:
  colour—red
  flowers—thistle, honeysuckle
  gemstone—diamond
  trees—thorn-bearing varieties
  food—traditional rather than exotic.

sign: TAURUS

dates: 21 April to 21 May

origin and glyph: the bull's head, which
has links with early civilizations in
Egypt.

ruling planet and groupings: Venus;
feminine, fixed and earth.

typical traits: Taureans rely upon stability and security, both in an emotional and financial context, but
granted this they can be extremely reliable, patient

and tenacious. They tend to be persistent, methodical and see things through to the end, and this can be reflected in their steady progress through life, including their career. Their lack of flexibility can often lead to resistance to change, even when it is for the better. However, when facing the challenge, they usually cope better than most. Taureans are practical people who dislike waste, and they tend to have high standards.

en famille: a good partnership is important to Taureans, and this means a happy harmonious partnership. Their need to put down roots and build can render them very good at making a home, as does the practical side of their character. They usually make good husbands and wives, and parents, but they may make the mistake of getting stuck in a rut. One of the faults of Taureans is jealousy and possessiveness, which can often be applied to a partner.

Having established a good home, Taureans will probably consider children to be very important, and the parents will strive to make their children happy. Babies and toddlers can be slow to reach the obvious milestones such as walking, but in later childhood things need to be learnt only once. Discipline is important because Taureans are essentially traditional and look for rules and guidance.

business: although Taureans do not like taking risks,

they are ambitious. However, they are more likely to stay with a job than to chop and change, and will quite possibly remain in uninteresting employment because the income is well nigh guaranteed. Sure handling of money and financial affairs comes easily to Taureans, and many find careers in the financial sector.

wider aspects: routine is vital, and change or uncertainty makes them uncomfortable. They enjoy leisure pursuits but must guard against becoming too lazy.

associations:

colour—pale shades, especially blue, pink and green

flowers—rose, poppy and foxglove

gemstone—emerald

trees—apple, pear, ash

food—generally like their food.

sign: **GEMINI**

dates: 22 May to 21 June

origin and glyph: two children, from Castor and Pollux of Classical mythology, which are bright stars.

ruling planet and groupings: Mercury; masculine, mutable and air.

typical traits: these include such characteristics as

liveliness, versatility and intelligence, but these are tempered to some degree by a nervous energy and a certain inconsistency at times. They are logical, ordered and very quick of mind, seeking variety in their lives, both at home and in their work. They tend to be good communicators but at times let their desire to communicate dominate all else. They can take in information very quickly if they are concentrating enough, but run the risk of knowing a little about a lot rather than grasping one topic in great depth. This is not necessarily a bad thing, of course.

en famille: the Geminian curiosity and versatility render relationships a little more prone than most to disruption or diversion. However, partnerships can last, particularly if the husband/wife finds an interesting companion with whom he or she can interact intellectually. Gemini women often marry men who can deal with domestic chores, as such women have no love of housework.

As parents, they can be lively and creative but sometimes over-critical. It is not uncommon for Geminians to make poor parents because they can be too impatient, too heavily involved in their own careers and over-competitive, seeking reflected glory in their children's achievements.

Gemini children are likely to talk and walk relatively early, and it will be necessary to keep them

well occupied. It is often advisable to encourage
them to finish anything they have started, to ensure
numerous tasks are not left in various stages of com-
pletion. Because Geminians can also be quite cun-
ning, and although they may be very able at school,
they can often put their own thoughts before hard
facts.

business: Geminians are very good when dealing
with money and can, therefore, be admirably suited
to banking or accountancy. As might be expected,
the ability to communicate and the lively personality mean they may also fit well into employment in
some aspect of the media or advertising. The pitfalls
inevitably are that attention to detail may be lacking
and that there must be variety. Conversely, they handle pressure well and are good at handling several
tasks at once.

wider aspects: change and variety remain of para-
mount importance, whether in leisure pursuits or re-
tirement. Individualism will dominate over group
activities, which may become routine.

associations:

colour—yellow, although most are liked

flowers—lavender, lily of the valley

gemstone—agate

trees—any tree producing nuts

food—salads and fruit, fish.

sign: **CANCER**

dates: 22 June to 22 July

origin and glyph: the glyph represents the breasts; Cancer probably came from ancient Babylon.

ruling planet and groupings: Moon; feminine, cardinal and water.

typical traits: the protective nature of the Cancerian is the overriding aspect of the character, but it is tempered by a stubborn and often moody streak. Although they tend to be of the worrying type, Cancerians have a remarkably good intuition, and their instinctive reactions and decisions can usually be relied upon. There is, however, a changeability about Cancerians that manifests itself in several ways. They can rapidly adapt to pick up information, habits, etc, from others. It also means that they can be touchy and, like the crab, may be hiding a soft, easily hurt person beneath a seemingly hard shell.

en famille: the caring nature of Cancerians makes them excellent at building a home and good at forming long-lasting partnerships. In general Cancerians like to look back in preference to forwards and commonly stay in the same house for a long period of time. A slightly negative aspect is that their protective nature can become excessive and turn into clinging, and they may be touchy and occasionally snap for no apparent reason.

The sensitive almost retiring aspect of the character can be seen quite early in life, and this may continue to the point that they become very shy at school; they may hide behind a shell. It is commonly the case that Cancerians will eye new social contacts somewhat warily, keeping them at arm's length. However, when they get to know each other better, firm friendships can develop.

Cancerians usually like their extended family within a reasonably short distance and are keen to help anyone who may need their support.

business: Cancerians can turn their hand to most things, and their careful, intuitive approach can make them successful. They tend to work well with people and often adopt the role of mediator, where diplomacy is required. The caring professions (for example, medicine) are obviously well matched to the Cancer character, but teaching may also be suitable. Although business may prosper under a Cancerian, there is often a tendency, even a fear, to change, which may show itself as inflexibility.

wider aspects: Cancerians are extremely sensitive, and while outwardly they appear charming and friendly, they can be temperamental and subject to wide mood swings. In general they love change, and while travel appeals, home has the greatest attraction.

associations:

colour—silver and pastel shades

flowers—white flowers, especially the rose, lily

gemstone—pearl

trees—none in particular

food—dairy foods and fish.

sign: **LEO**

dates: *23* July to 23 August

origin and glyph: it probably originated in ancient Egypt, from the constellation; the glyph resembles the lion's tail.

ruling planet and groupings: Sun; masculine, fixed, fire.

typical traits: Leonians tend to be generous, creative and yet proud individuals who nevertheless need to keep a tight rein on themselves to avoid becoming overbearing. The creative nature needs to find an outlet in whatever guise, and it is common for Leonians to become organizers, with confidence and energy, although beneath that they may be rather nervous. The possible risk is that Leonians may end up taking over and feel they always know best, so they must learn to listen to the views of other people. They can also display a temper, if only briefly, and are prone to panic if things go badly wrong. However, they generally regain control of the situation quickly. Their impatience and tendency to go over the top are countered by the abundance of their positive qualities.

en famille: to their partners Leonians will be affectionate, but their strong will and urge to lead can make them rather domineering. However, they can be very sensitive, and criticism can cut deeply. As parents, Leonians understand and encourage their children and will do anything to ensure they are not unhappy. However, they are not over-compliant and often associate with traditional values when it comes to behaviour and education.

Leo children tend to have an outgoing and bright personality, but they must not be allowed to be bossy towards other children, nor must their stubborn streak be allowed to develop. However, any criticism must be levelled in such a way as not to dent the rather fragile Leo self-confidence.

business: whatever their occupation or position, Leo individuals will work hard, in part because they are happier when they have people working for them. For many, luxury or glamour will appeal, and if they can achieve this through their employment then so much the better. As such, they may turn to acting,

sport or working in the jewellery trade. They will
often go for highly paid jobs, which they equate
with status, but, equally, they make good employers, expecting the best of their employees but generous in return.

wider aspects: the Leonian is better leading rather
than following and excels where generalities rather
than attention to detail are accepted.

associations:
  colour—gold and scarlet
  flowers—marigold, sunflower
  gemstone—ruby
  trees—citrus, walnut, olive
  food—honey and cereals, most meats and rice.

sign: **VIRGO**
dates: 24 August to 22 September
origin and glyph: the Egyptian god-
  dess of grain (Nidaba) was probably
  the origin, and in old pictures the
  Virgin is shown bearing an ear of corn and holding
  a child; the glyph is the female genitalia.
ruling planet and groupings: Mercury; feminine,
  mutable and earth.
typical traits: Virgoans are traditionally shy and
  modest, hard-working and practical and yet, perhaps, rather dull. They have a well-developed ten-

dency to criticize both themselves and others, and often allow this to go too far. If a positive tenor is applied to Virgoan traits, it results in someone who works hard, is sensible and intelligent, and very good at detailed tasks.

Being essentially a worker, Virgoans are not interested in taking the lead but more in completing a task to the best of their ability. There is a likelihood that Virgoans will be worriers, and they often worry about nothing at all, which can be misconstrued or counterproductive. However, their own positive qualities are the best tools to deal with such problems.

en famille: Virgoans are very loyal in relationships and fond of their family, although this love may not manifest itself openly but rather in private. They may be self-effacing or even devalue themselves by feeling unworthy. A more common fault would be to over-criticize, but in the main they are caring, sound partners.

Children like to be kept occupied and at school will be neat, tidy and helpful. Their natural shyness may make them seem aloof, but if they can build up their self-confidence this will help them to keep worry at bay.

A great deal of time and attention will be paid to the home to keep it nice, but care should be exercised so that standards are not kept too high.

business: as already mentioned, Virgoans are not particularly ambitious and therefore are happier when supervised at work. If attention to detail is required then they are very capable and proficient in problem-solving or working in science or medicine. Although they like to be appreciated, they are happier working as a member of a team. They have an incisive style, useful in the media and the teaching profession.

wider aspects: there is a desire for purity, perfection and happiness, which, provided that their self-esteem is strong enough, is attainable through application of their own qualities.

associations:

colour—grey, green, brown

flowers—bright small flowers, e.g. buttercup

gemstone—sardonyx (a white/brown banded variety of onyx)

trees—nut producing varieties

food—root vegetables.

sign: **LIBRA**

dates: 23 September to 23 October

origin and glyph: The element of the scales may have several origins, possibly from their use

origins, possibly from their use in weighing harvests; the glyph is similar to a yoke.

ruling planet and groupings: Venus; masculine, cardinal and air.

typical traits: Librans are true to their origin—they are always trying to achieve a balance, whether between views, negotiating parties, or in their own environment. In many instances, because they prefer not to take one side or the other, they sit in the middle, and this indecision can be their greatest fault. Turned to positive effect, by combining their desire to balance with their undoubted charm, Librans make fine 'diplomats' and can often settle an argument to everyone's satisfaction. They are also easy-going and like quiet surroundings at home or work, but although they may appear vulnerable, they are in fact quite tough and ensure that they follow their own plans.

en famille: in relationships with a partner, Librans can be complete romantics and regard this relationship as very important, so much so that even the Libran indecisiveness can be overcome for a time. They tend to fit well into the domestic scene, being quite capable of organizing the household with their usual equable approach to all things, including money.

Librans make kind parents, although they must ensure that they are strong-willed and insist upon children doing as they are told. The Libran indecision might irritate some children, and every effort should be made to answer a child's queries. Children with this Sun sign tend to be charming and affable, and are often popular at school. Indecision and laziness should be identified and wherever possible overcome.

business: as mentioned, the tact and evenhandedness of Librans make them ideal as diplomats, in public relations, or any profession requiring these qualities. Their appreciation of art and beauty lends itself to a career in the arts or literature, and fashion, beauty and related professions are all possibilities for them. Although they like to work with other people, especially those of a like mind, they are sufficiently ambitious to reach for the top, although any isolation that this might produce would be unwelcome.

wider aspects: Librans work well anywhere where there are pleasant surroundings that are well ordered.

associations:
  colour—blues and pinks
  flowers—bluebells, large roses
  gemstone—sapphire
  trees—ash, apple
  food—cereals, most fruits and spices.

associations:
  colour—deep red
  flowers—dark red flowers such as geraniums
  gemstone—opal
  trees—thorn-bearing varieties
  food—foods with strong flavours.

sign: **SAGITTARIUS**
dates: 23 November to 21 December
origin and glyph: the origin is unknown,
  but the glyph, represents the arrow of the
  Centaur.

ruling planet and groupings: Jupiter,
  masculine, mutable and fire.
typical traits: Sagittarians are essentially gregarious,
  friendly and enthusiastic, with a desire to achieve all
  goals that are set. They are rarely beset by depression, but their inborn enthusiasm can sometimes
  take them too far, and they may take risks. Although
  they are versatile and intelligent, their desire to
  jump from the task in hand to the next in planning
  may result in some tasks being unfinished. In excess,
  their good qualities can become a nuisance, leading
  to tactless, hurtful comments (without the intent to
  hurt) and jokes that go a little too far.
en famille: freedom is important to Sagittarians, so
  much so that it may inhibit long-standing relation-

ships. After settling down, however, they are good in the family context, and their enthusiasm can help lift boredom or depression. Most Sagittarians will enjoy a friendship or partnership more if they are given a loose rein to enable them to do what they want. Often their ultimate goal is not materialistic but more spiritual.

As parents, this approach to life means that they encourage their children to be outgoing, and this is fine providing a child is not nervous or shy. The natural enthusiasm of Sagittarian children should be guided to productive ends, and their instinctive dislike of rules should be dealt with diplomatically if they are to reason. There is considerable potential in the child who has a gentle guiding hand upon him or her.

business: as already mentioned, Sagittarians are not interested primarily in material gain and because they are particularly interested in education and travel, that is where money may be spent. Work of a varied nature is preferred, but care should be taken to make sure details are not omitted in the race to move on to something new. There is a natural desire to help others, which may manifest itself in a career in teaching, counselling, lecturing, the Church, law, and even publishing.

wider aspects: when both mind and body have a cer-

tain degree of freedom, Sagittarians are at their best
and will then employ their versatility and intellectual strengths to the full.

associations:
  colour—purple, deep blue
  flowers—carnations
  gemstone—topaz
  trees—oak, ash, and birch
  food—good food is enjoyed but caution must be
  employed to avoid overindulgence. Specifically
  currants and the onion family.

sign: **CAPRICORN**
dates: 22 December to 20 January
origin and glyph: it may have originated with a mythical sea-goat from
  ancient Babylon. The glyph, is said to
  represent a goat's head and a fish's
  tail.
ruling planet and groupings: Saturn, feminine,
  cardinal and earth.
typical traits: it is said that there are two types of
  Capricornian, one of which has greater and higher
  hopes of life. In general, they are patient and practical and can be very shy, preferring to stay in the
  background rather than be in the spotlight. Even
  though they may be retiring, they are strong-willed

and can stand up for themselves. Capricornians often have a reputation for being mean, and for being ambitious and rather hard people. A mean streak may often be directed at the self, and ambition, if tempered with realism and humour, can be a positive trait. It is usually the case that the character is enhanced by other elements of the chart to produce a warmer personality.

en famille: Capricornians make good partners, although they may come late to marriage to ensure a career has been established and that the correct choice is being made. Once set up, they are likely to be happy and to provide well, if economically, for the family. This aspect of caring can extend well outside the immediate family, and although there may be a lack of confidence, a Capricorn subject will not allow him or herself to be pushed around.

As parents, they are serious but sometimes can be too strict. However, they encourage their children and will make sacrifices elsewhere to assist their child's progress.

Capricorn children may be a little slow to develop but usually come into their own eventually. They are very loyal and benefit from a secure background, which offers discipline, but at the same time they should be helped to build up their self-confidence.

business: although they make very good back-room

people, Capricornians can also do well leading from
the front and in their own businesses. Many have an
affinity for scientific work and can pay attention to
detail when necessary. They are good when working
with people, although they tend to have rather an
isolationist attitude, taking advice only grudgingly.
One might well find them in local government, fi-
nance, publishing, building or politics.

wider aspects: those with Capricorn as their Sun sign
are generally happy alone in leisure pursuits and
therefore enjoy music, reading, etc.

associations:
  colour—dark colours
  flowers—pansy, ivy
  gemstone—amethyst
  trees—pine, willow
  food—starchy foods, meat.

sign: **AQUARIUS**
dates: 21 January to 18 February
origin and glyph: there are several
  links with the water carrier, and the
  glyph clearly resembles water waves,
  although the similarity to serpents has also been
  noticed.
ruling planet and groupings: Uranus; masculine,
  fixed and air.

typical traits: Aquarians are renowned for their independence and the fact that they like to operate according to their own rules. This can lead to them becoming very stubborn, which should be overcome, but they can be inspiring because they do not easily lose hope. Aquarians are friendly, although they may not be totally reliable when circumstances become difficult, and highly creative in terms of ideas. However, they are not necessarily sufficiently practical to see through the ideas. Overall, they may be a little perverse or paradoxical, but beneath it all is a gregariousness and a real wish to help.

en famille: because of their independence, Aquarians may find it difficult to establish an emotional tie. However, providing they find the right type, who is not weak but capable and sensible, personal relationships can be very successful. They are usually totally faithful.

With children, they are supportive but may find it difficult to cope with emotional problems. Children may be a little unconventional, and some school environments may not be conducive to the full development of their potential. Parents of Aquarian children should be aware of this. On the positive side, children will be originators, naturally friendly, and show the Aquarian traits of creativity and an affinity for science. The natural friendliness should not,

however, be allowed to develop into a trust of anyone, particularly strangers.

business: not surprisingly, Aquarians like the freedom to do whatever they want, and they tend not to
heed anyone who tries to boss them around. They
are highly inventive and are generally good with
any subject of a technical nature. They are also
highly competent at practicalities. This makes for a
considerable range of occupations, and Aquarians
often turn their hand to science, communications,
teaching, social work and general administration.

wider aspects: Aquarians are by their very nature a
little out on a limb and unconventional, but their
very positive qualities make this an interesting Sun
sign.

associations:
  colour—electric blue
  flowers—orchid
  gemstone—aquamarine
  trees—fruit trees
  food—a light diet suits best, including fruits.

sign: PISCES
dates: 19 February to 20 March
origin and glyph: there are numerous links
  between the two fishes and various deities
  from history, including Jesus Christ. The

glyph represents two fish, linked, but also refers to the physical and spiritual side of the person.

ruling planet and groupings: Neptune; feminine, mutable and water.

typical traits: the Piscean person is really quite sensitive but above all is a highly sympathetic and caring person who invariably puts other people first, especially the family. They have great intuition and are good at understanding the needs of other people and make very good, kind friends. Sometimes they can take their idealistic and self-effacing stance too far, resulting in an unwillingness to face decisions, and sometimes they will rely on other, stronger, characters to lead for them. They are usually always tactful but should beware that helping others and becoming involved emotionally is not always a good thing.

en famille: in partnerships, Pisceans can be a little difficult to cope with, but with the right partner will help to build a welcoming home. They like visitors and to visit others, and their self-sacrificing attitude means that they will usually go a little bit further to make people happy, or an occasion just right. It is important that their lack of strong will is not exploited by a stronger character.

Pisceans love children and make very good parents providing they are not too 'soft'. They do have an inner strength, and can be very tough and resource-

ful if the occasion demands it and when they rise to
the challenge. Children often take second place to
others and may need some help with their self-confidence. However, they can be very good in science
and with parental encouragement can be good
achievers.

business: it is not surprising, with their caring in-
stincts, that Pisceans make good teachers and members of the health and related professions. They tend
not to be particularly ambitious but can have extremely good business minds. Success is usually
more likely if they have a supportive business partner. Other professions that often attract Pisceans include acting, the ministry, and anything linked with
the sea.

wider aspects: Pisceans have to be careful that in
helping and caring for others they tend to ignore
their own pursuits or problems.

associations:

   colour—sea green

   flowers—water lily

   gemstone—moonstone

   trees—willow

   food—excesses should be avoided, salad foods are
   very suitable.

The Chart

All the foregoing is background information that helps in the interpretation of a birth chart or horoscope. A typical blank chart is shown below. The solid central line represents the horizon and the numbered segments are the houses, as described previously. On this chart are plotted the positions of the Sun, Moon and planets.

To begin with, the following information about the subject is required:

—the date of birth,
—the time of birth and whether it was British Summer Time or not, and
—the place of birth and the appropriate latitude and longitude.

From the information, the position of the ascendant and midheaven can be plotted, followed by the planets' positions. As each planet is placed on the chart there will be certain angular positions developed between them, and when these form specific

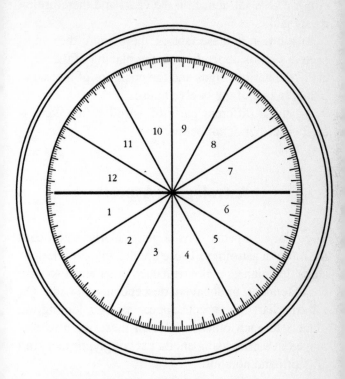

Figure 5: The Birth Chart

angles they are called *aspects*. These aspects have considerable influence on the chart and therefore on its subject.

In addition to these factors, there are further interpretive factors depending on the placing of the planets in the various signs and the positions of that same planet in one of the twelve houses.

All these different parts of astrology are considered in further detail below.

Astrological Aspects

The word 'aspects' has a particularly significant meaning in astrology. These are the angular relationships that planets make with each other and also with the ascendant, midheaven, descendant and nadir. On a birth chart the aspects appear as lines joining the planets to each other, and often these are also displayed in a grid, using another set of glyphs in a kind of shorthand notation.

Aspects form a qualifying statement about the planets and, depending on their effect, can be called easy or difficult, or, alternatively, the degree of their effect may be classed as positive, negative or weak. Hence, some aspects will make life easier for the subjects while others will introduce difficulties. Other factors should also be taken into account, namely the nature of the planets concerned and the houses and signs in which they occur.

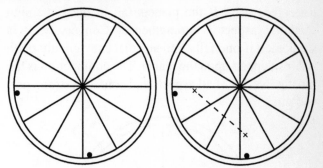

Figure 6: Constructing Aspects

An aspect is considered valid only if the respective planets are within a certain number of degrees of each other. The width or range allowed is called the *orb*, and, not surprisingly, an exact aspect is much stronger than a wide one. There is some difference in the size of the orbs used by different astrologers, but major aspects commonly have an orb of 8 degrees while others are 4 degrees, and for those aspects with only a minor influence, the orb may be 2 degrees.

The different aspects with appropriate glyphs are listed below, starting with the *major aspects*:

Major aspects

Conjunction ♂ can be positive or negative.

A conjunction is when two planets or a planet and the ascendant are located close to each other (within the 8 degrees orb). If the planets fall in the same sign then the aspect is strengthened. Conversely, it is weakened if one falls into an adjacent sign, although it does depend upon the planet. The conjunction is the most powerful of all aspects and confers a strong personality.

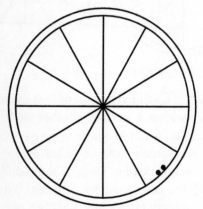

Figure 7:Conjunction

Opposition ♂° is negative.

Opposition is when two planets are opposite each other, within the orb of 8 degrees. This is also a powerful aspect and can indicate problems in dealing with people or handling different facets of the personality.

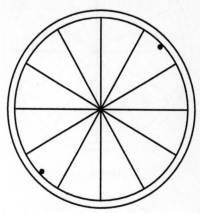

Figure 8: Opposition

Trine Δ is positive.
A trine is formed when two planets are 120 degrees apart and in general indicates that the planets work well together. (*See* figure 9).

Square □ is negative.
When two planets are 90 degrees apart, a square is formed. This is quite a powerful aspect but may represent tension, disruption or difficulties, although it can equally be put to positive ends. (*See* figure 10).

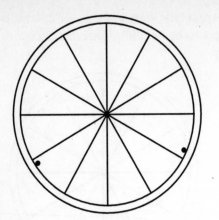

Figure 9: Trine

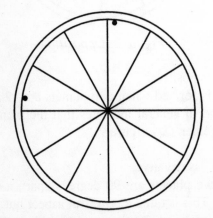

Figure 10: Square

Sextile ⚹ is positive.
The sextile marks two planets or features that are 60 degrees apart. Like the trine, the sextile indicates a helpful, easing influence, although it is not as strong as the trine.

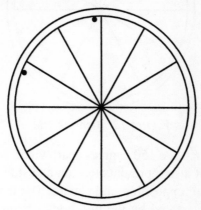

Figure 11: Sextile

Medium aspects

Semi-sextile ⚺ is weak to negative.
The semi-sextile is formed when there are 30 degrees between the two planets, and it represents tension and slight stress. (*See* figure 12).

Quincunx ⚻ is negative.
The quincunx (otherwise called the *inconjunct*) is

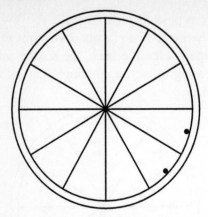

Figure 12: Semi-sextile

when planets are 150 degrees apart within an orb of 2 degrees. It also represents tension and stress but less so than the opposition and square. The tendency to tension is created by the two bodies being in signs that have no relationship with each other through triplicity, quadruplicity, etc. It can be very difficult to live with. (*See* figure 13)

Minor aspects
Semi-square ∠ is negative.
If the angular separation between planets is 45 degrees, a semi-square is formed. Since it has some connection with the square, it generally represents difficulties. (*See* figure 14)

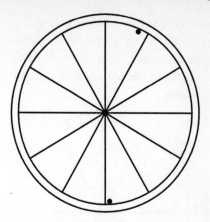

Figure 13: Quincunx

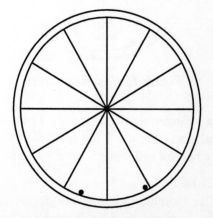

Figure 14: Semi-square

Sesquiquadrate ⬙ is weak to negative.

The sesquiquadrate, or *sesquare*, is when an angle of 135 degrees separates the planets. Again it has obvious connections to the square and accordingly represents difficulties.

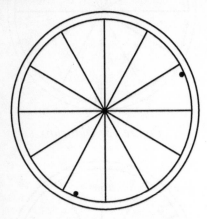

Figure 15: Sesquiquadrate

Quintile Q

This is a strange angular aspect of 72 degrees. It is very weak and little used, but is meant to indicate a generally helpful influence.

Biquintile BC

This is like Quintile Q but of 144 degrees. It is also very weak and little used but is meant to be a generally helpful influence.

Parallel ||
When planets are the same measurement above and below the ascendant from each other, they are said to be parallel.

Aspect patterns
When a chart has been plotted with all the information, certain aspects will become apparent. By joining up the information in a particular construction, certain patterns are formed that have influence upon the subject's personality, and they can work to his or her benefit or detriment.

Upon establishing a particular aspect, a point is made midway between the centre of the chart and the planet on the periphery. Lines then join these points for each aspect, creating a chart with several geometric shapes that are discussed below. It is often the case that different aspects are drawn with different lines (solid, dotted, dashed, etc) or several colours are used to help differentiate between oppositions, trines, sextiles, and so on.

There are a number of *aspect patterns*, which may involve three or four planets. It is generally the case that all the planets form aspects. If, however, there is an unaspected planet it will be a very powerful feature but may represent personality problems. The main aspect patterns are:

Tee-square

This configuration consists of two planets in opposition with a third that makes a square aspect to both of the other planets. All the aspects so constructed are negative, but it often confers strength. A great deal depends upon the planets involved, but it can be a forceful, dynamic subject with this pattern.

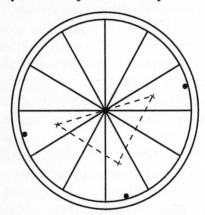

Figure 16: Tee-square aspect pattern

Grand trine

The grand trine is a triangular aspect formation with three trine aspects. At first sight this is a positive aspect, but it does depend greatly on other factors. For example, there may be a tendency to laziness and weakness of character, and if more than three planets make up the trine, there is the tendency for the element that is highlighted to become too strong. Charts should be studied carefully, however, as there are often other patterns that compensate. For example, the presence of a tee-square pattern will add some solidity and strength to the character.

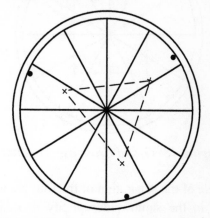

Figure 17: Grand Trine aspect pattern

Grand cross

The grand cross is not a common feature, but when it does occur it forms a very strong influence. It is made up of four planets in a four-cornered square such that there are two oppositions comprising planets at opposite corners. In addition, the four planets make square aspects with their adjacent planet. The result is that it is a very powerful feature and can be disruptive, although its effect may be lessened by other aspect patterns.

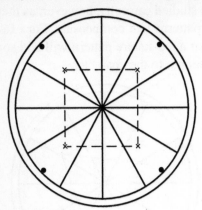

Figure 18: Grand Cross aspect pattern

Because of the separation of the four planets, each will fall in the same quadruplicity or quality, i.e. fixed, mutable or cardinal. This confers a slightly different perspective on the interpretation.

The *fixed grand cross* suggests an individual who may be stubborn or at least someone who tolerates the *status quo*. It may be that he or she has been put upon and criticized so much that he or she has given up.

The *mutable grand cross* implies adaptability and potentially an ability to overcome obstacles and work around problems. There may still be nervous stress because although the subject will opt for an easy solution and a straightforward life, other factors may prohibit this, such as a feeling of duty.

The *cardinal grand cross* essentially implies a desire and a will to overcome difficulties. A lack of self-confidence may prove a barrier, but, with sufficient determination, this can be overcome and result in considerable achievement.

Pointer

A pointer aspect pattern is made up of two planets in opposition and one of these two then forms quincunx aspects with two further planets, producing a pattern shaped like an arrowhead.

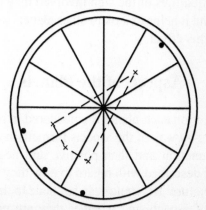

Figure 19: The Pointer aspect pattern

The quincunx and opposition are both indicative of tension and stress, and this is compounded by two semi-sextile patterns at the other end of the pointer. Overall, then, this is a stressful pattern, and in many cases it focuses, at its point, on the house of importance.

Stellium

A final pattern that may occur is when three or more planets occur in one house or sign, and this implies a reinforcing of the concerns of the house or the characteristics of the sign. This arrangement is called a *stellium*, and can cause a certain imbalance in a subject's chart because of the emphasis it applies. The extreme qualities of the sign involved may be accentuated, and it helps to look to other planets to counterbalance this effect.

Aspects of the Planets

In this section each planet is considered in relation to the others by way of the aspects formed. In each case the conjunction and then positive and negative aspects are described with regard to how they affect the overall picture. Reference can be made to the preceding list of aspects and whether they are positive or negative.

The Sun

Aspects made by the Sun to other planets are very important in interpreting charts, and planets aspected to the Sun will be strengthened. The effect of the planet or planets on the Sun shows how its own influence will be manifested. If the Sun aspects with the ruling planet of the chart then it is very important.

Sun/Moon aspects

In conjunction these planets generally confer harmony, and there is an emphasis on characteristics associated with the sign. The conjunction may not always be in the same sign or house. If this happens, it may reflect an inner conflict normally associated with negative aspects. Positive aspects between the Sun and Moon represent a coherence and oneness of the personality, while negative aspects mirror the likelihood of unsatisfied restlessness. Minor aspects will have little influence and will have a subsidiary role in the presence of other features.

Sun/Mercury aspects

Because the Sun and Mercury are never more than 28 degrees apart, the only aspects that can occur are a conjunction or semi-sextile. If the conjunction is close, less than 5 degrees, it is customarily taken that the subject will be a slow developer, although experience does not necessarily confirm this. In general these aspects confer an energetic and positive outlook. If the planets are in the same sign, the subject will think and express himself or herself in the nature of that sign.

Sun/Venus aspects

The Sun and Venus are never more than 48 degrees apart, so the only aspects possible are a conjunction, semi-sextile and semi-square. A conjunction represents affection, and the individual will probably enjoy the pleasurable aspects of life, often to excess. Other characteristics that may be strengthened or emerge are kindness and gentility, but, to excess, the overall result can be laziness and a certain irresponsibility. The semi-sextile will never be a strong feature, but it does indicate creativity and an appreciation of finer things, for example, art or music. If the semi-square occurs, it can indicate a rift in personal relationships.

Sun/Mars aspects

If the Sun and Mars occur in conjunction, there is a very strong positive, and cumulative, effect. Because of the individual effects of these planets, Mars for physical energy and the Sun for vitality, this conjunction is particularly forceful. This may also apply to the emotional picture of the individual. The bold, brave traits may be taken to the point of heroism but may equally result in overwork. Positive aspects have much the same effect but with a beneficial outcome and without treading on anyone's toes. Negative aspects include angry outbursts but more commonly the bad effects of overwork.

Sun/Jupiter aspects

In many ways a conjunction of the Sun with Jupiter can be regarded as highly fortuitous. It represents a general contentment, but more, people with this conjunction are held to be very 'lucky' as they will probably have considerable good fortune and opportunities in life. There tends to be a feeling that good luck can be expected. The outward-looking and expansive nature associated with Jupiter can result in an ambitious, intelligent and humorous individual. Positive aspects will have much the same result, and although the individual may not be particularly competitive strength may be seen in certain sports.

Negative aspects may include conceit, impudence and extravagance and a tendency to exaggerate, although these may be lessened to some extent if there are other, steadying influences in the chart.

Sun/Saturn aspects

It has been understood for some time that Saturn has a dampening effect on the Sun, cancelling out to some extent its vitality. Thus, in conjunction, Saturn will cause the Sun's effect to be limited and the cumulative result will depend very much on other planetary aspects. If other aspects are mainly positive then the effect of Saturn will be limited. Positive aspects introduce patience and a practical outlook on life, and although there may be shyness, it can be overcome.

The negative aspects are often manifested in a lack of self-confidence, and this may result, with other factors, in a tendency to ill health.

Sun/Uranus aspects

The Sun in conjunction with Uranus can be extremely strong and result in someone who is rebellious or rather eccentric. It may, however, also confer originality and independence, and there is often a scientific ability. Positive aspects can have similar effects, with a leaning to leadership, flashes of inventive thought and even genius. There is a greater emotional and nervous energy, which can sometimes be seen in a somewhat erratic enthusiasm.

Negative aspects are manifested as awkwardness and stubbornness, and the subject can be difficult, although this may be lessened by other factors.

Sun/Neptune aspects

In conjunction this aspect shows sensitivity and an

intuitive nature. If there are no negative aspects influencing the chart, there may well be a creative flair. There can, however, often be a tendency towards the impractical, and the individual may be thought of as having his or her head in the clouds. Positive aspects create a vivid imagination that can be used to good effect, but it may also verge into daydreaming and thus become less productive than it might be.

Negative aspects may produce vagueness and muddled thinking and quite often there is a deceitful aspect to the nature, whether it applies to the self or others. The daydreaming feature of such individuals may become a definite drawback in that issues and reality are avoided.

Sun/Pluto aspects

A conjunction between the Sun and Pluto can tend to produce obsessive behaviour and considerable self-analysis. Depending on where the conjunction falls, however, it can enhance an intuitive individual. Positive aspects reinforce the theme of self-analysis, and this may be extended into an ability to undertake research.

Negative aspects, on the other hand, may prove very frustrating, with a likelihood of the individual being very reticent to talk through problems and situations, even with family members and close friends.

Obsession is never far away but can be countered by other influences, particularly involving Venus and the Moon.

The Moon

Planets aspecting the Moon are subtly altered, and any matters ruled by that planet will probably undergo changes and modest alterations, heightening or lessening a particular characteristic.

Moon/Sun aspects—see section on **The Sun.**

Moon/Mercury aspects

A conjunction between the Moon and Mercury has a marked, positive mental effect, resulting in good instinctive behaviour that can extend into an active mind producing a facility for writing or something similar. Positive aspects produce common sense and the ability to work out a problem or situation and choose a logical solution.

Negative aspects can lead to a restless mind and an acrimonious nature, and although intellectual powers are heightened they may be used negatively, for example, in more gossip and criticism.

Moon/Venus aspects

The Moon in conjunction with Venus is a particularly good aspect, resulting in a balanced person who is calm, friendly and popular. It also has a positive effect on partnerships, making the individual very aware of his or her partner's needs. Positive aspects will show the same characteristics exhibited by a conjunction, with the additional benefits of intuition and charm.

Negative aspects may cause some difficulty in the outward expression of affections, and this can result in troubled relationships.

Moon/Mars

The conjunction with Mars produces a strong influence and results in a tendency to be direct and energetic. However, it can also render someone too quick, and liable to jump first and check the ground afterwards. Positive aspects result in good physical and emotional strength, which means that the individual can make progress, whether in work or life generally.

Negative aspects lead to moodiness and a tendency to quarrel and also an impulsive nature that may lead to the necessary rescue of hastily made decisions.

Moon/Jupiter aspects

In conjunction these planets confer a helpful, kind nature to the individual, who is generally optimistic about events and often has a relatively trouble-free journey through life. Positive aspects have the same effect, particularly the trine, and the mental faculties are enhanced.

Negative aspects create a slightly destructive slant to these qualities so that the nature may be essentially the same, but judgement is affected and gains may be squandered.

Moon/Saturn aspects

A rather serious, cautious and even pessimistic outlook can be engendered by a conjunction between these planets. There is a desire for order and for things to be correct, so much so that the individual may be tagged a perfectionist. There may also be a timidness to the character and an underlying feeling of inadequacy, but loyalty can be relied upon.

Positive aspects include a commitment to duty willingly given and an ability to work reliably, thereby gaining a good reputation that is usually rewarded with progress. A lack of self-confidence, shyness and difficult relationships with the opposite sex all reflect negative aspects. If the individual is not careful it is quite easy for depression to take over, and other aspects of the chart should be studied to find more positive, constructive influences.

Moon/Uranus aspects

If the Moon and Uranus are in conjunction, there will be tension and emotions may be strained. Alongside the quite scintillating effects that may occur, there is a perversity and desire for the unusual, and often an independence in behaviour. Positive aspects result in a strong intuition and a need to achieve, which can be channelled constructively in almost any direction. Mood changes are common but are usually for the better.

Tension, an overpowering will, frequent (if only temporary) disagreements with friends all reflect the negative aspects. Flair and creativity may be present, but they need to be handled in the correct way.

Moon/Neptune aspects

Idealism, sensitivity and kindness all reflect a conjunction between the Moon and Neptune. These can be so dominant in the make-up that it can work to the subject's detriment should others take advantage of him or her. It is important to avoid deceptions that may be perpetrated in order that others are not hurt.

Positive aspects frequently add imagination to the character, but this must be controlled to avoid a muddled approach. A seriously muddled mind is typical of a negative aspect, as is the non-fulfilment of positive traits.

Moon/Pluto aspects

A conjunction between the Moon and Pluto commonly produces someone who is changeable and prone to highly emotional outbursts. Even so, this may act to his or her benefit in that a fresh start can be made uncluttered by bubbling discontent. It may, however, prove no easy task for the individual to express his or her true feelings if other planets restrict the conjunction.

Positive aspects create a similar tendency; outbursts may occur but can ultimately prove beneficial while the need to 'clear the decks' every so often will enable something or someone to be exorcised from the person. Negative aspects result in an inability to express oneself and open up emotionally, which can be frustrating and ultimately destructive unless countered elsewhere in the chart.

Mercury

Since Mercury is the planet of the mind, communication and general mental capacity, it is often feasible to find a positive outlet in this area.

Mercury/Sun aspects—see section on **The Sun.**

Mercury/Moon aspects—see section on **The Moon.**

Mercury/Venus aspects

In conjunction there will be an ease of mind rather than worry and a harmony and understanding of other people. A pleasant manner and charming

speech result in good abilities to communicate. These
planets are never separated by more than 76 degrees
so the positive aspect that may be found is the sextile.
This results in a friendly and affectionate nature and
often an appreciation of, and ability in, craft pursuits.

The negative aspects may be the semi-sextile,
which is very weak (and thus of little consequence),
or the semi-square. The latter similarly has little adverse effect, save perhaps a critical manner, but depending on the configuration it may actually produce
a greater balance of emotions in the character.

Mercury/Mars aspect

In conjunction with Mars, Mercury takes on the
forceful, energetic nature of this planet. This produces someone who is mentally sharp, decisive and
agile and able to take decisions quickly. Such individuals will probably prove effective in discussion or
debate, which may serve them well in business. Ag-
gressiveness may appear but will usually be manifested in strong opinions that the individual is quite
happy to voice. Positive aspects produce much the
same results with a lively mind but in addition an
ability to handle stressful situations.

Negative aspects may result in moving too quickly,
resulting in premature action, and incisiveness can
become a more destructive carping. The mental fac-

ulties can be overloaded, resulting in tension and even a breakdown.

Mercury/Jupiter aspects

This conjunction confers very good mental creativity and potential, which may reflect a writer or any sort of literary occupation. There tends to be an appreciation of broader concepts rather than fine detail, although this will depend to a certain extent upon the remainder of the chart. A cheerful optimistic individual with a sense of humour reflects positive aspects, and in such cases challenges are necessary to stimulate the mind and obtain the best. Otherwise there may be a tendency to laziness.

In general, the negative aspects are not particularly problematical, but there can be carelessness if the mind is overloaded, or a tendency towards absent-mindedness.

Mercury/Saturn aspects

The conjunction of these two planets has a contradictory effect in that there is a mix of communication and limitation. It creates someone with a serious and thoughtful perspective on life, but he or she can become pessimistic. If combined with a good chart, there will be common sense and an attention to detail; conversely, a bad combination can result in mental slowness. Saturn will also inhibit and limit positive aspects, but there is often an enthusiastic nature combined with a useful reliability.

Negative aspects may force these characteristics to excess, causing obsessive behaviour in many ways, such as orderliness, self-discipline and depression.

Mercury/Uranus aspects

This conjunction is a particularly dynamic one and leads to a very quick mind, rich in inventive and innovative thought. It may also impart independence and a little stubbornness, and can produce an unconventional character who prefers the unusual and unorthodox. This is also seen with positive aspects, leading to originality and inventiveness, especially in a scientific context. Such individuals are self-assured and may be good with their hands.

The ability to communicate may become too sharp and almost isolated under the influence of negative aspects, and reaction to delays or difficult situations may be quite out of proportion to the problem faced. The preponderance of following the unusual can seem to others to be eccentric, which in itself becomes counterproductive.

Mercury/Neptune aspects

Mercury and Neptune in conjunction produce a fascinating result. The sensitivity and inspiration of Neptune confer on the individual a highly flexible mental attitude, resulting in creativity, intuition and a fertile imagination. There will not, however, necessarily be the rationalizing effect of common sense, and this may result in daydreaming. Positive aspects have a similar effect—sensitivity, kindness and an intuitive feel for people's aspirations and even thoughts.

Negative aspects lead to gullibility and unwillingness to face reality, and the thinking may operate in a scheming, deceptive way.

Mercury/Pluto aspects

The conjunction of Mercury with Pluto produces an individual capable of dispensing with worries easily and someone who enjoys the mental challenge of solving a mystery. A similar vein is seen with positive aspects, and there is a fascination and thoroughness when dealing with a topic that has once caught the individual's interest.

Negative aspects tend to be manifested as a secretive nature, perhaps with obsessive or stubborn sides to the character.

Venus

In general any planet aspected by Venus will be softened, resulting in an enhancement of certain characteristics, such as the expression of love and dealing with possessions.

*Venus/Sun aspects—see section on **The Sun**.*

Venus/Moon aspects—see section on **The Moon**.

Venus/Mercury aspects—see section on **Mercury**.

Venus/Mars aspects

These two planets have a limiting effect on each other when in conjunction so that Mars limits the delicate beauty of Venus, and Venus limits the robust, coarse nature of Mars. As a result, the individual is enthusiastic, while sensitive to a partner's needs and also able to enjoy sexual relationships and all things of beauty. Positive aspects work in much the same way, with the further introduction of warmth into relationships.

Negative aspects may increase tension in relationships, often resulting in hurt and quarrels. If Venus is the stronger planet then the subject may be oversensitive to the comments of others.

Venus/Jupiter aspects

A conjunction between Venus and Jupiter is a very beneficial aspect and confers popularity, an artistic inclination and an affectionate nature. Such individuals work better in partnerships rather than alone and may lead a busy love life. Positive aspects produce similar results, and the individual will be popular, charming and happy.

Negative aspects tend not to be too detrimental because of the beneficial nature of both Venus and Jupiter. In most cases it will be an excess of a particular characteristic, thus the charm will be overplayed or an excessive number of love affairs will cause problems or there may be a discontent with being alone.

Venus/Saturn

When Venus is in conjunction to Saturn there is often some factor that inhibits the complete and open expression of affection or love, and this may produce disappointment in such affairs. There may also be a strong sense of duty, which, although it may bring its own rewards, can be traced back to strong inhibitions. Positive aspects tend to be less restrictive than the conjunction, and while there is a serious side to relationships, a particular partnership can benefit from faithfulness.

Negative aspects are also restrictive, to the point where it is difficult to express affection, although more positive characteristics elsewhere in the chart may help overcome this barrier.

Venus/Uranus aspects

In conjunction, these planets confer an element of inconsistency and an inability to focus the attention. In addition, emotions and tension may run high, and this really needs to be channelled and controlled. Although considerable personal appeal is possible, commitment may be lacking. Positive aspects lead to a less compulsive and magnetic personality and a tendency towards creativity and often considerable achievements.

The personality may retain its magnetism and dynamism, but under the influence of negative aspects there may also be a dramatic temper and impatience, which can cause nervous tension and strain.

Venus/Neptune aspects

There is a sensitivity and idealism when Venus is in conjunction with Neptune and an inclination towards pleasant or amiable behaviour. If the subject lives too much in the clouds, however, there will be self-delusion and a likelihood that partnerships and associations are not as solid and secure as perceived. When positive aspects are found, these will increase the chance of success, particularly in artistic pursuits such as music. Ideas and hunches may occur during periods of apparent daydreaming, but in many cases these can prove more realistic than at first believed.

Negative aspects can produce problems, in that restlessness can turn to discontent if other areas of the chart reinforce this trait. There is a possibility of self-delusion unless common sense appears elsewhere, and confusion can occur in personal relationships.

Venus/Pluto aspects

The conjunction of Venus with Pluto is often a powerful one when it comes to emotions. It is quite likely that love will be felt deeply and passionately, but unless it is reciprocated there may be upheavals. Both planets influence money affairs, so this area may form a theme for a career. Positive aspects produce a very similar effect on personal relationships, especially those of the heart, while negative aspects tend to block these factors. The emotions may well be present, but there is an inability to talk above them and this can lead to frustration.

Mars

Mars will strongly affect any planet it contacts and will tend to create extremes in its positive and negative aspects.

Mars/Sun aspects—*see section on* **The Sun.**

Mars/Moon aspects—*see section on* **The Moon.**

Mars/Mercury aspects—*see section on* **Mercury.**

Mars/Venus aspects—*see section on* **Venus.**

Mars/Jupiter aspects

A conjunction between these two planets has very strong effects, resulting in energetic, decisive, enterprising individuals who tend not to miss opportunities. In addition, they will probably be willing to take on challenges that others would not even consider. There is a tendency for individuals to be almost daring, although they may be more argumentative. The influence of positive aspects is very good, leading to good humour, enthusiasm and the constructive taking of opportunities, whether physical, material or intellectual. Unless it is countered by controls shown elsewhere in the chart, the negative aspects can be quite destructive, with excesses in action and thought.

Mars/Saturn aspects

There tends to be something of a conflict when these planets are in conjunction, with Saturn limiting and Mars enlivening. As a result there may be mood swings from determination to frustration, from gloom to optimism. There may also be obstinacy. Positive aspects create a slightly more harmonious character such that the individual will be very determined. If put to good use this can lead to achievement in certain fields.

Negative aspects tend to result in a stern attitude, but this also means that hardships are endured. Selfishness is another trait that may be seen.

Mars/Uranus aspects

The combination of Mars and Uranus in conjunction

produces very strong attributes, with determination, often obstinacy and frankness. Although this may not make the most pleasant of individuals, there will be a desire and ability to reach goals, but there may also be undue haste, which can result in accidents. Positive aspects confer independence and a magnetic character, but this may be a disadvantage unless used well. Flair and creativity can be manifested in engineering or science.

Tension and nervous strain result from negative aspects, and an argumentative nature is very likely. Personal relationships may be strained or broken because of tactlessness, and an awareness of other people's feelings has to be engendered.

Mars/Neptune aspects

The conjunction of Mars with Neptune stimulates the imagination and strengthens the emotions. It can also make the individual somewhat lazy. In general there tends to be an interest in the arts, dancing and similar pursuits. Positive aspects lead to a creativity and original thinking that would be well employed in design. The emotional side of the individual is also enhanced.

Negative aspects can all too often result in escapist ways that can lead to problems. There may also be moodiness, and hard work undertaken possibly for perfectly altruistic motives may come to nought, perhaps because the idea had little substance at the outset.

Mars/Pluto aspects

An almost explosive nature can result when Mars is in conjunction to Pluto. Certainly there will be a determined, stubborn outlook, and it may be necessary to find a controlled outlet for the excessive energy. The temper is likely to be fierce, and obsessions are always possible. The character may even be flawed by a cruel streak. Hard work and ambition characterize the positive aspects, even to the point of the subject becoming a 'workaholic'.

Because both energy and emotions are increased by negative aspects, the subject may become someone who works almost obsessively to achieve a goal.

Jupiter

Jupiter's influence tends to be one of expansion and the provision of greater scope, and is often associated with understanding and knowledge.

*Jupiter/Sun aspects—see section on **The Sun**.*

*Jupiter/Moon aspects—see section on **The Moon**.*

*Jupiter/Mercury aspects—see section on **Mercury**.*

*Jupiter/Venus aspects—see section on **Venus**.*

Jupiter/Mars aspects—see section on Mars

Jupiter/Saturn aspects

The conjunction of Jupiter with Saturn brings together seemingly opposing principles of limitation and expansion. If the influence of each is balanced, then common sense, a balanced approach to life and positive thinking will result. If the influences are not balanced there can be swings between optimism and pessimism, but in any event there is usually application to the task in hand and the ability to stay to the end. Positive aspects emphasize the constructive combination of common sense with optimism, producing a rounded character for whom little cannot be achieved. The intuition is good, as is their ability to plan and bring ideas to fruition.

Negative aspects introduce dissatisfaction and restlessness allied with a lack of self-confidence. There is also a tendency to press on regardless, even when caution is called for.

Jupiter/Uranus aspects

This conjunction produces an individual who is positive in his or her thinking, independent, and with a considerate approach to others. There may also be a good sense of humour, and such people are unlikely to be lost in the crowd. Many of these features are also produced by positive aspects, but in addition there is determination, self-belief and possibly an eccentricity bordering on genius.

Eccentricity can work to the individual's detriment under negative aspects, with an associated streak of pomposity. Such an individual may consider that everyone is wrong except he or she.

Jupiter/Neptune aspect

In conjunction these planets convey a kindness and desire to help others combined with idealism, although the effect of the latter trait will be shaped by the rest of the chart. In general there is optimism, and while there is a tendency to dream, a practical side should be sought. The positive aspects tend to be quite similar in effect, with an added altruism in their efforts.

The negative aspects often result in the beneficial qualities of kindness and sensitivity being overridden by lack of attention. In the extreme there may be escapism, foolishness or deception.

Jupiter/Pluto aspects

Jupiter in conjunction with Pluto produces a desire for power, material gain and an obsession in attaining goals. If it goes too far, it may verge on the fanatic, but if controlled these traits can prove very beneficial. The individual may well show leadership potential, and there may well be prominence in life at some time. Positive aspects provide similarly useful features, such as determination, the ability to lead and organize, and great strength of character.

The fanatical side of a character can develop under negative aspects, and if this is combined with an ability to lead and draw people, problems may arise. There may be a compulsion to gain what is wanted by violent means and to break away from existing constraints. Such tendencies must be tempered.

Saturn

A key feature of Saturn is its limiting effect, and this possibly relates to its being at the edge of the universe until late into the eighteenth century when the 'modern' planets were discovered.

Saturn/Sun aspects see section on **The Sun.**

Saturn/Moon aspects see section on **The Moon.**

Saturn/Mercury aspects see section on **Mercury.**

Saturn/Venus aspects see section on **Venus.**

Saturn/Mars aspects see section on **Mars.**

Saturn/Jupiter aspects see section on **Jupiter.**

Saturn/Uranus aspects
This conjunction has very great potential and, de-

pending on the position of the conjunction, can result
in great achievers. A practical outlook combined with
persistence and other beneficial aspects can create
brilliance. In certain circumstances the aspects can
combine to produce someone with true leadership
qualities, possibly a leader of their generation. There
could always be nervous tension because of the conflict between limitation and freedom, which has to be
countered. A balanced, perhaps more integrated,
whole is generated by positive aspects, with persistence, patience and yet originality.

With negative aspects there may be a conflict, producing a stubborn nature and someone who is awkward and has a tendency to suffer from nervous tension.

Saturn/Neptune aspects

The conjunction of these two planets is interesting in
that Uranus lies between the two for this period of the
last generation, and this has a considerable effect.
The overall result is an individual with a strong character who has ideas and imagination but controls
them to the greatest benefit for all. There is a similar
result with positive aspects, and in addition there is a
kind and caring nature. An aptitude for science is not
uncommon.

Negative aspects render these traits weaker, leading to confusion and a lack of application. There may be self-deprecation accompanied by shyness.

Saturn/Pluto aspects

Aspects involving these two planets occur rarely and last a long time when they do happen. The conjunction occurred last early in the 1980s when both planets were in Libra. This results in a determination allied with a pushing drive. Positive aspects confer a more determined outlook and also stubbornness.

Obsessional behaviour is typical of any negative aspects, and there is a tendency to avoid facing problems through misplaced fear, which makes the individual appear to waste time.

Uranus

Aspects between Uranus and the remaining planets Neptune and Pluto stay within orb for a long time (for example, from 1989 to 1998) because of the immense distances and separations involved and also the slow movement of Uranus. This means that such aspects will apply to the charts of people born within a long period.

Uranus/Sun aspects see section on **The Sun.**

Uranus/Moon aspects see section on **The Moon.**

Uranus/Mercury aspects see section on **Mercury.**

Uranus/Venus aspects see section on Venus.

Uranus/Mars aspects see section on Mars.

Uranus/Jupiter aspects see section on Jupiter.

Uranus/Saturn aspects see section on Saturn.

Uranus/Neptune aspects

In conjunction there is the combination of independence, imagination and intuition with sensitivity, which produces an individual with inspirational qualities. Positive aspects often result in creatively or scientifically gifted people because logic, flair and similar attributes are strengthened.

Negative aspects may result in nervous tension, and the individual may be rather absent-minded. In such cases it is good practice to seek compensatory traits and activities elsewhere in the chart.

Uranus/Pluto aspects

This conjunction occurs very infrequently, roughly once every 115 years, and because of the slow relative movement of the planets the effects are relevant for a generation. In many charts it will therefore not be a particularly strong feature. However, it may result in general frustration within the house in which the conjunction falls. Positive aspects may result in a likelihood to seek change while negative aspects can result in this trait being overdone and leading to disruptive behaviour.

Neptune

The majority of cases in which Neptune aspects with other planets have been covered in the preceding pages under the other planets. Just one planetary aspect remains.

Neptune/Pluto aspects

Because of the relationship between these two planets, conjunctions were formed many years ago but now Neptune is ahead of Pluto in their respective orbits around the Sun. As such a conjunction will not occur for some considerable time.

The only aspect that Neptune makes with Pluto is the sextile, and this occurs quite a lot in charts. Depending on the general construction of the chart, this may have little effect or it may strengthen intuition. However, the sextile is a weak aspect as other factors will tend to override it.

Aspects to the Ascendant and Midheaven

Other aspects that are important in interpreting charts are those between the planets and the ascendant and midheaven. In general, those to the ascendant have a personal implication while to the midheaven the implication applies to self-expression. It is essential that an accurate time of birth is known to allow a full interpretation. If this is not known, aspect to the ascendant and midheaven are better not included. The primary features and possibilities of these aspects are summarized below.

Sun/Ascendant aspects

Conjunction rounded character, amiable; could be domineering, reticent.

Positive depends on house position, but usually a strengthening effect

Negative depends on house but can be ambitious. Love of home but can be problematic

Moon/Ascendant aspects

Conjunction moody and often easily influenced. Secretive but intuitive.

Positive good intuition, common sense with an adaptable character

Negative impatient and often discontented.

Mercury/Ascendant aspects

Conjunction mentally sharp, versatile and communicative. Likely to be imaginative.

Positive	similar to the conjunction.
Negative	tense and prone to worry and be over-talkative.

Venus/Ascendant aspects

Conjunction	affectionate and loving with an appreciation of things artistic. Care necessary not to overdo food or drink.
Positive	similar to the conjunction, with an understanding nature.
Negative	this may cause excesses in behaviour and personal relationships.

Mars/Ascendant aspects

Conjunction	a strengthening of physical or emotional energy. May be selfish but can be altruistic.
Positive	physically active, independent.
Negative	prone to quarrelling. May overdo things,for example, in work.

Jupiter/Ascendant aspects

Conjunction	depending upon the house, can be optimistic and lively but also fair-minded. May be a risk-taker.
Positive	effects similar to the conjunction.
Negative	may be prone to showing off to the detriment of relationships.

Saturn/Ascendant aspects

Conjunction self-consciousness; practical with common sense nevertheless. Can be moody but also content, particularly in the home surroundings.

Positive common sense and practical nature; also cautious.

Negative may be pessimistic with a tendency to complain.

Uranus/Ascendant aspects

Conjunction original and independent but can be irrational. There may be nervous tension.

Positive lively and creative usually with a need for independence.

Negative unpredictable and possibly melodramatic.

Neptune/Ascendant aspects

Conjunction variable effects but may include creativity, ill-discipline, or irrational behaviour.

Positive quite inspired but may be tempered by forgetfulness.

Negative possibly self-deceptive, and blinkered in situations where logic and analysis might be more appropriate.

Pluto/Ascendant aspects

Conjunction strong emotions. May be secretive and prefer being or working alone.

Positive   can be precipitate in actions; caution is required.

Negative   desire for change may become strong.

Sun/Midheaven aspects

Conjunction ambitious and hopeful and usually self-confident. Can also be 'too big for their boots'.

Positive   ambitious but in a constructive way.

Negative   difficulty in achieving, great effort required.

Moon/Midheaven aspects

Conjunction a strong character with possibility of leadership qualities.

Positive   a strengthening of traits associated with the sign containing the midheaven.

Negative   a dissatisfaction with life; dashed hopes or unfulfilled dreams should be overcome with encouragement.

Mercury/Midheaven aspects

Conjunction highly communicative, can be applied to a career.

Positive   similar to the conjunction, also a
               balanced view of objectives.
Negative   may be prone to tension and worry.

Venus/Midheaven aspects
Conjunction works well with people; considerate;
               may not have full powers of concentra-
               tion and organization.
Positive   similar to the conjunction; more con-
               structive effect than the conjunction for
               self-employed.
Negative   can be arrogant; prone to overreacting.

Mars/Midheaven aspects
Conjunction thirst for success; energetically pursues
               the career.
Positive   enthusiastic, particularly in work.
Negative   hard-working but may be argumentative.

Jupiter/Midheaven aspects
Conjunction content and optimistic; usually popular
               and fair. Can be successful, usually
               enthusiastic in whatever venture is in
               hand.
Positive   good at meeting challenges, which
               enhances self-esteem. Optimistic and
               enthusiastic.

Negative usually successful in a career but may exaggerate, thereby losing standing with people around.

Saturn/Midheaven aspects

Conjunction ambitious and can be high achievers; can handle responsibility but may let other aspects of life pass them by.

Positive common sense and practicality; a good worker, who looks for promotion but reckless.

Negative may experience frustration in reaching for goals; can be self-conscious and too cautious.

Uranus/Midheaven aspects

Conjunction independent, perhaps with an inclination to rebellion, but may be creative and clever. Changes of direction possible, as is a liking for control.

Positive similar to the conjunction, but with an innovative quality. The urge to change should be tempered, as it may become detrimental.

Negative tension and a resultant over-caution may impede progress.

Neptune/Midheaven aspects

Conjunction changes in direction may become
                frequent although this will not neces-
                sarily restrict progress.
Positive   imagination and flair will help appro-
                priate careers.
Negative   liable to deceive, the subject may use
                dubious methods to achieve his or her
                aims.

Pluto/Midheaven aspects

Conjunction a desire for influence may predominate.
                Careers may be marked by sudden,
                quite remarkable, changes of direction.
Positive   an ability to handle unexpected change.
Negative   life may throw up challenging situa-
                tions with which some will cope and
                others not. It will all depend upon the
                remainder of the chart.

Other aspects

In addition to considering the aspects formed between planets, there are other factors of importance,
such as the house position, that is, where the Sun,
Moon and other planets fall with respect to the
houses and what this contributes to the interpretation.
Before moving on to this facet of chart interpretation,

the next section describes the basic procedure in drawing up a birth chart.

Constructing the Birth Chart

The construction of a birth chart is essentially a fairly elementary mathematical exercise. There are computer programs that enable it to be done simply, but in undertaking the task manually there is greater understanding and achievement.

Before beginning, a number of items are required:

—a blank chart; the one shown here is of the equal house system (*see* figure 5 on page 89). It can be drawn up quite easily using a pair of compasses.

—pen, pencil and ruler (and to begin with, probably an eraser).

—an atlas for determination of longitude and latitude.

—access to Raphael's ephemeris, which provides data on the position of the planet by month and year. Also known as the ephemerides, they are contained in some astrological books or you may have to consult a library. They are also available on computer.

—detailed instructions to follow or a computer program to use.

The following stages provide an overview of the process involved without complicated guidelines. It shows essentially how the data is derived but allows us to concentrate on the interpretive aspects of the subject.

Stage 1
The central horizontal line marks the horizon, and starting in the house below this line, the houses can be numbered 1 to 12, moving in an anticlockwise direction.

Stage 2
The position of the ascendant is now calculated. There are a number of calculations to be made, but the first task is to determine the longitude and latitude of the place of birth. The time of birth is also vital and should initially be stated as the birth time in Greenwich Mean Time. To find the ascendant and midheaven, the birth time is converted to sidereal time (that is, in relation to the stars) with minor adjustments for the year. Because the sidereal time from the tables relates to midnight it must be changed to the sidereal time at the time of birth by adding the sidereal time to the time of birth. Again, minor amendments have to be made at this point, both for minor changes in sidereal time and the precise geographical

location of the place of birth. Again, tables are used for this latter correction. This calculation produces a true sidereal time of birth, and by referring to a *table of houses*, degree values can be found for the ascendant and midheaven.

In this example the ascendant is 22 degrees Cancer and the midheaven is 20 degrees Pisces. Referring back to the chart, the 22 degrees are counted clockwise around the chart from the horizon line and the ascendant is marked. This is the cusp (that is, junction) of the first sign, and the remaining sign divisions can be drawn in from here, every 30 degrees around the chart. The glyphs of the sign are then added and the midheaven is also positioned.

Stage 3
The next stage is to determine the positions of the Sun, Moon and other planets. By reference to the ephemerides, the positions can be found, and these are given as a number of degrees in a particular sign. The example here results in the following, rounded to the nearest degree for simplicity:

Sun	13 degrees	Cancer
Moon	11 degrees	Sagittarius
Mercury	9 degrees	Leo
Venus	17 degrees	Cancer
Mars	5 degrees	Scorpio

Jupiter	15 degrees	Taurus
Saturn	9 degrees	Libra
Uranus	14 degrees	Cancer
Neptune	19 degrees	Libra
Pluto	21 degrees	Leo

Each planet is now marked on the chart in the relevant sign, counting anticlockwise from the sign division. Each plot should be marked and the appropriate planetary glyph inserted. The chart, completed to this point (figure 20), is shown overleaf with all information calculated to date.

Stage 4

When the planetary positions have been established, the aspects can be determined. As described earlier, there are various aspects that may be apparent, and when constructed as described their significance can be determined from the other sections of the book. On the sample chart there can be seen conjunctions (the Sun with Venus and Uranus), sextiles (the Sun, Uranus and Venus, all with Jupiter; Pluto with Neptune), squares (Neptune with Venus and the Moon with Saturn), and so on.

The complete picture of a chart, and the personality, is built up from information such as this but also the details gleaned from the position of the planets with respect to the signs and houses. The Sun's sign

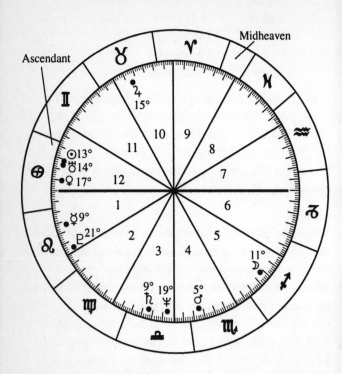

Figure 20: The Birth Chart with initial placings of the ascendant, midheaven and the planets

influence has already been covered in reasonable detail, and below the remaining planets are dealt with. It is possible to give only the briefest indication of influences here, but more comprehensive details will be found in other publications. The next section therefore deals with the planets through the signs and houses, beginning with the Sun through the houses.

The Planets through the Houses

The Sun
The energy of the Sun is very important, and it shows by its house position in which facet of life the energy will be focused.

The Sun in the . . .

. . . First house—indicates the strong, self-centred type who is good at giving orders—and may therefore be successful in business—but not so good at taking them.

. . . Second house—very acquisitive, both in terms of money and other possessions and with a desire to flaunt it a little. This may also apply to a partner, that is, the partner is also regarded as a possession. The

motivation may be a wish to be wealthy or a fear of being poor.

. . . *Third house*—at whatever level, the mind will be active and the person will be a communicator.

. . . *Fourth house*—seeks the security of a good home and happy family life, and may also work from home.

. . . *Fifth house*—creativity needs to be expressed and enjoyment will be gained from that. Spontaneous and proud but generous and may be upset easily. There is a desire to feel important and wanted.

. . . *Sixth house*—such people are hard workers and often commit themselves to the local community, or their employer and, of course, their family. Personal health is a feature of this house, whether for good or bad, but it may also show as employment or voluntary work in the health sector.

. . . *Seventh house*—relationships with others become very important whether it is on a personal level or concerned with work. Emotional dependence may actually become a problem.

. . . *Eighth house*—an interest in self-development,

which may relate to money or the personality. Strong emotional tendencies with a perceptive mind.

... *Ninth house*—education and travel are both associated with this house and both help to broaden the mind. There is a strong desire to learn and possibly to teach.

... *Tenth house*—a strong commitment to ambition, work (may actually overdo work) and possessions, with a desire for progress in a career. Secure family life is also important.

... *Eleventh house*—is drawn to cooperative ventures, working with other people and is often a good communicator. Very close relationships are however often avoided.

... *Twelfth house*—tends to like quiet and seclusion but can be creative. The most withdrawn of all the houses. Usually wants to improve life for others even though the subject may have no great ambition for himself or herself.

The Moon in the ...

... *First house*—a natural instinct to care for others

but not to the detriment of self-interest. Likes travelling. Is susceptible to mood changes.

... *Second house*—there is a need for security through money and possessions and often a desire to collect the latter. Emotions will affect judgement on money.

... *Third house*—usually a good communicator and often turns to teaching. Shrewd but could be a deceiver. Intelligent and humorous but commonly restless and always on the move.

... *Fourth house*—a strong feeling exists for the home and family and a safe, solid base is essential. Caring and protective in nature, but may become obsessive and retiring.

... *Fifth house*—an outlet for creativity is vital, which may manifest itself in parenthood. Socially active and may be something of an extrovert but with quick reversals of mood.

... *Sixth house*—good workers who often opt for charity work or the health field. Emotions frequently affect health and work.

... *Seventh house*—usually look for close emotional ties, although in so doing their individuality may be lost. Subject to mood swings. Job variety and interest is sought.

. . . Eighth house—emotional and intuitive, often to the point where they have a 'sixth sense'. Usually a good business sense. Strong sexual needs.

. . . Ninth house—an interest in things foreign, be it travel, language or culture. Also a tendency for higher education and for religion.

. . . Tenth house—an ability to lead and a desire for status and power. An understanding of those being led, which can lead to being highly esteemed.

. . . Eleventh house—tends to get involved in activities involving groups, which they themselves may lead. Politics commonly appeals.

. . . Twelfth house—time alone is always valued. In working for others it is usually 'behind the scenes'.

Mercury in the . . .

. . . First house—talkative and quick-witted with some nervousness. Versatile and keen to learn and to present own ideas. May be prone to excessive worry.

... *Second house*—financially astute with an aptitude for financial dealings and the creation of wealth.

... *Third house*—usually communicative and often employed in a profession where such skills can be used. Mentally agile with an interest in education.

... *Fourth house*—the home is particularly important and may base work there. Interest in the family and its past and history generally. Can be restless.

... *Fifth house*—highly creative in a literary or craft pursuit although may be lacking in attention to detail. Generally at ease with children, something that is usually reciprocated.

... *Sixth house*—excellent at communication and in analysing situations and problems. Makes a good employee, working carefully, and also a good employer who maintains an interest in employees, their health, etc.

... *Seventh house*—seeks a sharing, caring relationship whether in marriage or pastimes. Can be a good business person with an ability to act as intermediary. Often interested in other's problems but not necessarily out of totally altruistic motives.

... Eighth house—may have an interest in mysterious things, for example, psychic phenomena, but can also prove to have a good business sense. An enquiring mind with good powers of concentration.

... Ninth house—a thirst for knowledge and understanding is very strong and may lead to a career in research with considerable academic achievements. Also may have an aptitude for languages.

... Tenth house—variety is necessary, particularly in the career, and there may be changes in career direction. Generally a good approach to business, although financial reward is not necessarily the primary motivation.

... Eleventh house—a very friendly type who enjoys social contact and the opportunity to discuss ideas. This may lead to involvement in local groups, organizations or politics.

... Twelfth house—tends to be emotional and shy, almost secretive and lacking a little in self-confidence.

Venus in the ...

... First house—an attractive and charming character, which in part is a means to securing friendship.

Kind and sympathetic, often interested in the outward appearance, that is, fashion and beauty.

. . . *Second house*—likes to collect possessions, especially things of value and beauty. A competent approach to business in the main, but this is often used to impress.

. . . *Third house*—very friendly and sociable with an ability to communicate effectively. Welcomes a mental challenge.

. . . *Fourth house*—the home is central and is a focus of pride. Every attempt is made to make it nice and secure and comfortable. Dislikes arguments and can be quite effective at defusing situations likely otherwise to end in quarrels.

. . . *Fifth house*—likes luxury and glamour and participating in social events. Gets on well with children. Creative with an affinity for the arts.

. . . *Sixth house*—the working environment must be pleasing and conducive to work. A steady pace in all things is ideal. Socially correct and critical of those who are not.

. . . *Seventh house*—an interesting combination of

shrewdness and affection. Often popular with their peers, they can sometimes rely too much on a partner and make unreasonable requests.

. . . *Eighth house*—an increase in emotions and sexual matters can be uplifting or totally problematic. Generally sympathetic but can become jealous and secretive.

. . . *Ninth house*—a strong interest in other cultures with a desire for foreign travel, which may lead to residence or even marriage abroad. Varied contacts in social circles with a relaxed attitude in general.

. . . *Tenth house*—socially adept with positive spin-off in the career, forming good relationships with work colleagues.

. . . *Eleventh house*—large number of social contacts and an enjoyment of communal ventures, fund-raising, etc. Good organizer of events.

. . . *Twelfth house*—shy and incommunicative with secretive emotional feelings.

Mars in the . . .

. . . *First house*—very energetic and positive although sometimes impulsive and even hot-headed. They usually put themselves first although can be very helpful to others.

... Second house—a desire to build up possessions and wealth but often an extravagant spender. Very competitive in business and may be likely to take risks.

... Third house—competitive and often argumentative. Also inquisitive and may have a temper. In being argumentative, they may also lack tact.

... Fourth house—much effort is spent on the home in decoration and improvements. On occasion restlessness may precipitate moving home.

... Fifth house—energetic in all aspects of life— whether social, creative or romantic. A keen sportsperson who enjoys leisure time. Tends to be good with children but often pressurizes his or her own children to succeed.

... Sixth house—a hard worker who gets on with the task in hand. Quite ambitious and competitive but can be rather impatient when faced with delays. They will also be difficult when disagreeing with colleagues.

... *Seventh house*—forceful in partnerships and can prove argumentative. Can be popular through their energetic participation but they can offend or upset people through their outspoken nature.

... *Eighth house*—interest in investigative work or financial occupations. Highly intuitive. Strong sex drive.

... *Ninth house*—adventurous and interested in travel. Also intellectually very capable and may find education rewarding. Usually have strongly held views and beliefs.

... *Tenth house*—a very strong character and a hard worker, which in regard to the career means ambition, success and an achiever. Although they make good employers, they can on occasion be a little too ruthless.

... *Eleventh house*—likely to get involved in various groups and organizations where they will probably become leaders. Friends are important but their basically argumentative nature may cause temporary rifts.

... *Twelfth house*—a desire to help others, perhaps in the caring professions but often working behind the scenes. Can become secretive, too much so, which leads to problems not being discussed and solved.

Jupiter in the ...

... First house—honest, optimistic and generally outgoing with a tendency to offer encouragement to others. A possible weakness may be overconfidence.

... Second house—money is a central theme although the emphasis may vary. In some, money is made effortlessly while in others it is of secondary importance. Generous in partnerships and with a desire for comfort in the home.

... Third house—welcomes mental challenges, shares ideas and opinions but may force them on others. Can be restless but there is often a desire to continue in education, possibly through self-teaching.

... Fourth house—strong ties with the family and home life and may have ambition for a large house.

... Fifth house—enthusiastic and optimistic, and may also be creative. Generally self-confident but in excess this can lead to risk-taking and someone who shows off.

. . . Sixth house—helpful and generous and particularly so in work when a good rewarding job will take precedence over the financial return.

. . . Seventh house—friendly and quick to form new contacts, although sometimes with an ulterior motive. Good in business and assertive, with plenty of ideas for development.

. . . Eighth house—often a good business person who invests wisely. Can be over-demanding where a partner is concerned and may also like freedom to the detriment of a relationship.

. . . Ninth house—may have an interest in travel and foreign cultures. There is also a continuing desire to find out, acquire knowledge or study. Can become self-opinionated.

. . . Tenth house—an ability to grasp the significance of situations and take a long-term view. Tend to work towards their goals, becoming wiser en route. Can be rather melodramatic with a tendency to show off.

. . . Eleventh house—very sociable with many superficial friends and acquaintances, and just a few real friends. Quick to offer encouragement and provide ideas.

. . . Twelfth house—can be rather idealistic, finding the material world unsatisfactory. Prefer in many cases to work alone although they will have an excellent mind.

Saturn in the . . .

. . . First house—shy and lacking self-confidence although with common sense and responsibility. Can often meet with repeated setbacks but through dogged perseverance can succeed.

. . . Second house—works hard to make the money that is gained but little comes easily in this respect. There may be a tendency to possessiveness, and over-caution can lead to lost opportunities.

. . . Third house—success usually comes later in life through sheer hard work as a lack of confidence is overcome. Usually practical-minded and sensible with a caring attitude to brothers and sisters.

. . . Fourth house—a potentially unhappy early life may link at a later stage with the need for domestic security. Intuitive, although the individual may have to learn to accept intuitive judgements.

. . . Fifth house—a latent creativity may need to be

encouraged. May find dealing with children difficult, possibly because of their own childhoods.

. . . Sixth house—usually committed to hard work, although possibly in a complaining way, but goals are commonly met. Avoidance of change. May be excessively concerned about their health.

. . . Seventh house—regards partnerships very seriously and may choose an older partner, but tends to be very faithful. Occasionally there will be problems in relationships.

. . . Eighth house—a generally serious perspective on life, with the potential for depression. Very good at financial pursuits, particularly in their responsible attitude to the money of other people, thus suited to banking or insurance.

. . . Ninth house—thinks seriously and sensibly about important matters, but with a conventional, traditional approach to most matters. There is a tendency to travel, although in some this raises problems and even phobias.

. . . Tenth house—ambitious, with high hopes and an ability to take responsibility. These people make good, dependable workers who can progress through hard work, overcoming difficulties on the way.

... Eleventh house—hard-working and often a little shy. However, a definite effort may be made to be more sociable, which frequently results in membership of numerous committees. A concern for all good causes is evident.

... Twelfth house—can withdraw into his or her own world but in any event will welcome the security of home. Good, supportive workers in whatever they do.

Uranus in the ...

... First house—intelligent, freedom-loving and individualistic, so much so that they may prefer competition to cooperation. Quite unpredictable, but original and often brilliant.

... Second house—this has financial implications and may result in the unexpected gain or loss of money. Can be emotionally cool with a possessive streak.

... Third house—original and mentally alert and likely to respond negatively to the orthodox system of education. Seeks logical answers to problems, can

be inventive. A stubborn, awkward streak may also be apparent.

. . . Fourth house—a rather perverse, mixed-up influence with the subject wanting a stable secure home life but also considerable freedom. They may be brilliant but moody. However, it is best to encourage and develop the intuitive ideas of such a person.

. . . Fifth house—a creative individual with flair and originality. Their children tend to be clever but may be demanding. Emotionally rather fearless, these people will often take risks.

. . . Sixth house—may experience health problems, perhaps associated with tension. There is an affinity for work that is slightly out of the ordinary and that requires invention, flair or idealism.

. . . Seventh house—relationships are affected greatly. Often the individual will not want to be tied down and partners need to be very understanding. There may be mixed emotions about such ties that can lead to mistakes, although there can be a generally romantic outlook.

. . . Eighth house—commonly a relaxed attitude to

money, which may result in unpredictable actions that subsequently cause friction. Fickle sexually and possibly obsessive in analysing problems.

... *Ninth house*—often clever with a flair for science or the arts and an appetite for challenges. Travel is sought with possible attraction for a foreign culture resulting.

... *Tenth house*—career direction may change abruptly, particularly if there is not the scope for their talents. Not averse to holding positions of power, leadership is handled well.

... *Eleventh house*—superficially friendly with a varied social life and often a hard-working commitment to a cause or organization. Dislikes inaction and lethargy in others.

... *Twelfth house*—highly imaginative, often in a strange way with an interest in the unusual or mysterious. Often takes to a humanitarian cause to the detriment of a personal relationship.

Neptune in the ...

... *First house*—imaginative and sensitive with a

tendency to daydream. In general such people are kind and unselfish, but may be rather gullible.

. . . *Second house*—a potentially varied and unpredictable attitude to money including a susceptibility to be misled. May be sentimental and loving.

. . . *Third house*—imaginative and communicative, particularly with respect to artistic careers or pastimes. May achieve later rather than sooner through lack of application in the early years of education.

. . . *Fourth house*—chaos may reign at home in both organization and general provision of domestic routine but also in giving guidance to children. Usually imaginative and a lover of animals.

. . . *Fifth house*—creative, with imagination. Romantic associations can be a little too consuming and would benefit from a wise head.

. . . *Sixth house*—can be attracted to work in the caring professions but may not be very good at meeting deadlines. Tend to be self-sacrificing and often work hard for little recompense but can be impractical at times. Health may be a problem, particularly with allergies.

... *Seventh house*—too much may be expected romantically, and disappointment may result, or there may be a tendency to rush in without considering the implications.

... *Eighth house*—romantic/sexual activities can be quite dominant. In money matters there will be generosity, but the individual may prove easily led, perhaps by a business partner.

... *Ninth house*—inspired and imaginative with a fascination for other cultures and mysticism. May find a career in religion. Travel often features strongly.

... *Tenth house*—an idealist and romantic, which in a career can lead to unrealistic hopes or success if the idealism can be used to good effect. There are likely to be many changes of emphasis and direction in life.

... *Eleventh house*—sociable but not very perceptive in such circumstances. There may be some shyness and an aversion to taking on responsibility as this can result in stress.

... *Twelfth house*—kind and caring, which may be reflected in the choice of career where they can readily understand the problems of other people. Often creative with an affinity for the arts.

Pluto in the . . .

. . . First house—strong and dynamic with a determination to work hard and achieve targets. Can also be moody and obsessive with an emotional intensity. Strongly developed motivation with an excellent ability to bounce back after setbacks.

. . . Second house—there is usually a good aptitude for business and money matters, which when allied with a determination to succeed can lead the individual to considerable success. An intense emotional life, although may be manipulative.

. . . Third house—can be very good at communicating although often the urge to be quiet and contemplative masks this. Perceptive and curious, which may lead to a career in research.

. . . Fourth house—strong feelings about the home although there may be concealed frustration from his or her early life. Intuitive, and this will help deal with any emotional or family problems.

. . . Fifth house—usually creative and with a determination to use their potential to the full. Too much may be expected of romantic/emotional associations.

... *Sixth house*—a disciplined individual who works hard and to a routine if applicable and may be rather hard on himself or herself. May experience health problems.

... *Seventh house*—an aptitude for the financial aspects of a business. Can appreciate others, with understanding and sympathy, but must be careful not to dominate a partner.

... *Eighth house*—a good business sense. Intuitive and logical but may experience sexual problems.

... *Ninth house*—frequently shows connection with or interest in foreign countries and different faiths. Seeks mental challenge. Quite a strong personality.

... *Tenth house*—a strong desire to succeed, which may be shown in the career, where personal power will be sought. An interest also in money and politics. May be ruthless.

... *Eleventh house*—a tendency to become involved in groups or societies, and possibly in politics. There may, however, be a predominance of these interests over domestic concerns, to the detriment of the latter.

. . . *Twelfth house*—a likelihood that the individual
will be secretive, whether in financial or romantic
matters. Habitually searching and analysing, which
may be directed on themselves.

The Planets through the Signs

The positions of the planets with respect to the Zodiac signs are unique for each chart. Each planet has
twelve expressions through the signs, which follow a
basic pattern, so in Aries, planets act assertively and
powerfully.

The Planets in Aries
Moon—quick in reaction, thought and temper and
rather impulsive. Can be good partners but may also
be selfish.

Mercury—quick-thinking and strong-willed with an
enjoyment of debate. Decisive and to the point.

Venus—affectionate, even passionate, with a generous nature. Lively socially and generally popular.

Mars—energetic, even aggressive, and usually leading the way. They can be impulsive and obstinate although friendly, and they may create problems
through carelessness.

Jupiter—optimistic and enthusiastic with a love of freedom. Can be generous, but these traits to excess can lead to recklessness and extravagance.

Saturn—assertive and strong, and very determined, thus more than able to cope when circumstances become difficult.

Uranus—originality with self-confidence, although there may be impatience and a tendency to behave foolishly.

Neptune—this is an impossible placing because of the slow motion of Neptune.

Pluto—the same applies as for Neptune.

The Planets in Taurus
Moon—a solid base is required to counter any emotional ups and downs, but otherwise very practical with lots of common sense.

Mercury—stubborn but with an ability to consider problems of a practical nature and work steadily. Generally cheerful.

Uranus—warm and affectionate and generally faithful. Likes craft and the arts, including music. Aims for financial security, through hard work if necessary.

Mars—quick-tempered and passionate. Such individuals work very hard and can be very determined, almost stubborn. Works at making money.

Jupiter—appreciates good living and usually has the flair and good judgement to use and invest money well. Generous but can be possessive.

Saturn—very patient, with caution and discipline, but can become too stubborn. Ambitious and materialistic.

Uranus—stubborn yet sound and with some flair. May be erratic with money, splashing out and then saving every penny.

Neptune—this placing cannot occur for living subjects because of the slow orbit of Neptune.

Pluto—the same applies as for Neptune.

The Planets in Gemini
Moon—quick to respond and versatile. There is a reluctance to get too involved emotionally. Can be impatient and restless.

Mercury—a desire to communicate and exchange ideas. A quick thinker and decision maker and quite inventive. Can be impatient with slower people but adaptable.

Venus—a good communicator and a lively personality. Can be flirtatious but often avoids emotional ties through constant analysis and thus does not face the real issues. May be restless.

Mars—a good mind but has a tendency to take on too much, thereby reducing effectiveness. Usually versatile and capable but can be nervous and impatient.

Jupiter—inventive and clever but can skip from one area to another and grasp only superficial knowledge Often takes to teaching as communication is good.

Saturn—good mind with a logical approach to problems. May be a late developer and generally good at the physical sciences—computing, mathematics, etc.

Uranus—a quick thinker who has original and often brilliant ideas. However, he or she may be nervous and tense.

Neptune—very few people will have Neptune in Gemini, unless very old.

Pluto—applies only to the elderly (born before 1912).

The Planets in Cancer
Moon—highly instinctive, emotional and affectionate. A secure, stable home life is very important, and these individuals are adept at homemaking. Can be moody and a little possessive.

Mercury—kind and thoughtful with a good imagination. Intuition and opinions are strong, as is the dislike of change. A good memory is not unusual.

Venus—sympathetic and affectionate, but if overdone can be possessive and clinging. They love the home and make it as comfortable as possible and are likely to make sensible investments.

Mars—great commitment, physical and emotional, to see things through. Although they need security and a strong family life, they are ambitious. Occasionally very short-tempered.

Jupiter—kind and sympathetic, and also dutiful. Quite good at business and generally ambitious on behalf of and for the family.

Saturn—can be self-pitying and suspicious, and there is a need for emotional stability. May be a worrier, but there is also a financial aptitude and general shrewdness. Hard-working and ambitious.

Uranus—imaginative and original though logical. Can be moody and unpredictable and difficult to work with.

Neptune—this placing occurred in the early years of the twentieth century. It confers intuition and sensitivity although the individual may be too imaginative and prone to worry.

Pluto—generally emotionally strong and intuitive. Can be a good business person with staying power, although some may fall prey to excessive worry.

The Planets in Leo

Moon—confident and with a desire to impress, but can be self-centred. Enthusiastic and lively but may, in their ambition, start taking over. Can be stubborn and difficult.

Mercury—creative and well organized in a practical sense. A good communicator but can be arrogant and patronizing. Generally happy and with a positive outlook.

Venus—lively, generous and faithful, this person will adore his or her partner and will love children and material things. May be a tendency to show off and be extravagant.

Mars—looks for leadership because of organizational ability and enthusiasm. Socially active with a touch of drama that can be overdone. May be too pushy and overbearing.

Jupiter—usually generous and enthusiastic with a positive outlook on life. Can also be ambitious but melodramatic and overpowering.

Saturn—determined, well-organized and faithful ap-

ply here. Can often be bossy and arrogant, especially
if they are pursuing a long-held goal.

Uranus—quite dynamic, which can result in good
leadership qualities. However, there will almost certainly be stubbornness. Often creative but with mixed
personal outlook on relationships.

Neptune—enthusiastic and creative with a good imagination. Commonly an interest in the visual arts,
such as photography or film.

Pluto—may succeed in business through flair rather
than calculation. Interested in technology. Commonly shows leadership qualities although occasionally these may degenerate into empire-building tendencies.

The Planets in Virgo
Moon—a strong tendency to be well-ordered, neat
and with a dislike of bad behaviour. Can be lacking in
self-confidence and a worrier but with a practical
streak.

Mercury—an analytical mind and practical, which
makes these people good at solving problems. May
become bogged down in detail when wanting to be
precise but generally able to cope with demanding
tasks.

Venus—often shy and with few close friends, perhaps because they tend to be critical of other people, often due to their own lack of self-confidence. Good at business and communicating.

Mars—a hard worker who pays attention to detail but lacks imagination. The emotions and personal relationships may not run too smoothly.

Jupiter—patient but can be overconcerned with detail, critical but kind. There may be worry and mental conflict when facing a problem because of lack of self-confidence. Tends to be kind and matter-of-fact.

Saturn—patient, modest, with attention to detail and duty. Hard work is not avoided and personal standards are kept high. Can be too hard on others, for example, employees, and may be a little detached from others.

Uranus—can lead to originality but the familiar is not rejected. Depending upon other placings, the individual can be dynamic and somewhat restless.

Neptune—imaginative and expressive, but there may be a lack of self-confidence and an associated dissatisfaction.

Pluto—an ability to see, grasp and solve problems, although some individuals may find difficulty in talk-

ing about their own worries. Can be very critical of
others.

The Planets in Libra

Moon—sympathetic and understanding, to the point
where they will help to sort out problems for other
people. Clear thinkers, very charming but can be
moody.

Mercury—peace-loving, sympathetic, can see many
possibilities, but this can leave them indecisive. Gentle and affectionate. Often good at business but will
need application and discipline.

Venus—kind and understanding, and tactful in helping others with a dislike of argument. Quite generous
with money but fond of luxuries. May be lazy and indecisive.

Mars—affectionate, keen to promote and maintain
unity, but can themselves be argumentative. Perceptive and friendly.

Jupiter—sympathetic, kind and generous—a naturally warm person. Has a relaxed attitude to life with
a love of luxuries that can lead to self-indulgence.

Saturn—understanding with a feeling for what is
right and wrong, kind and fair. May be some intoler-
ance and difficulty with relationships.

Uranus—friendly and caring, and unselfish when someone is in need. May be independent and unsure of being committed to a partnership.

Neptune—sympathetic, peace-loving and kind. May be lacking in self-confidence and self-deceiving.

Pluto—a tendency to start arguments, particularly with a partner to prove a point. Can be jealous.

The Planets in Scorpio

Moon—very emotional and may be jealous. Determined with a strong ambitious urge. Tend to be a little retiring socially but in personal relationships can be very committed.

Mercury—intuitive with a logical mind although can be obsessional and possessive. Usually loyal in relationships.

Venus—passionate, possessive with occasional jealousy. Often a flair for business, investment and money, but obstinacy could interfere.

Mars—full of potential with a strong character. Hard-working with ambitions but self-discipline may be lacking. Perceptive with, occasionally, a critical nature. Can be secretive but with strong motivation and commitment.

Jupiter—determined, with a will to succeed, especially in the career. Lives a full life but in many cases may need to ease off a little.

Saturn—committed to goals, determined and with a very good ability in business. Can be ruthless, stubborn and obstinate, and consideration should be encouraged if they are to succeed.

Uranus—emotional but afraid to show it, courageous and may take risks. May be a liking for power but potential must be developed in the correct direction.

Neptune—emotional, but can be ambitious and even inspiring if this is also shown elsewhere in the chart. May be fortuitous with money.

Pluto—a desire to make money and achieve a powerful position in some way. Usually strong emotions and quite intuitive.

The Planets in Sagittarius

Moon—a liking for freedom and also travel, which may result in living abroad. A challenge is always enjoyed, and the individual is enthusiastic and positive with a desire to maintain progress. May be restless and a little offhand.

Mercury—can be unrealistic and superficial but, on

the positive side, will always be learning, and there is broad-mindedness. Grasps situations quickly, versatile.

Venus—emotional freedom is required, and may not like to be tied. Idealistic and imaginative but may be thoughtless.

Mars—very ambitious, often on a grand scale. Very energetic and independent but with a non-traditional approach. Can be argumentative and heavy-handed.

Jupiter—enthusiastic and positive with a tendency to look for intellectual development. Often intuitive and with a good sense of judgement.

Saturn—study is a primary aim, assisted by a capacity for concentration. Honest and forthright, these people will not be afraid to challenge the thinking of the majority.

Uranus—original in thought and welcomes a challenge, caring in an altruistic sense and with this is a good sense of humour.

Neptune—generally understanding and caring with an idealistic streak. Also enthusiastic and positive-thinking.

Pluto—this occurs only from 1995 until well beyond

the millennium. Likely to be independent and generally sensible, possibly wise.

The Planets in Capricorn

Moon—unable to show feelings easily and may find partnerships difficult although good at homemaking. Ambitious to some extent but with a tendency towards arrogance, but with a good sense of humour.

Mercury—down to earth, practical and to the point. Determined and careful, but can be restless. Often a tendency to scientific pursuits.

Venus—tends to stick with tradition and conventional relationships. Good in business with a careful approach, although occasionally showing off.

Mars—very ambitious, seeking targets, and with a liking for power. Generally practical-minded but can be stubborn and cold.

Jupiter—a good worker who sees the job through. Very sensible and responsible, with ambition and reliability. Can be stubborn.

Saturn—ambitious and practical, hard-working and well-organized. May like power. Can be pessimistic and likely to complain, but has a good sense of humour.

Uranus—a careful thinker but with occasional

lapses. There may be a hard side to the character, which could be tempered by a concern for good causes.

Neptune—possibly creative. Determined and positive with a cautious streak but may be subject to self-deception.

Pluto—it is unlikely that this placing will be found.

The Planets in Aquarius
Moon—independent, dislike of being tied down emotionally and may reject the responsibilities of a home. There is a strength of character but also an awkwardness and unpredictability. Often original with a flash of brilliance.

Mercury—like freedom, both physical and intellectual. Tend to be intuitive and inventive, often with radical views. May be stubborn and critical but very good with humanitarian causes.

Venus—tends to value freedom, even in personal relationships, which can cause problems. Kind and caring and usually good with money.

Mars—original thinker and intellectual but can be impulsive. Idealistic but more often than not impractical. Can be erratic and stubborn.

Jupiter—imaginative, evenhanded, idealistic and

fair. Such people have many good qualities, such as understanding, warmth, cheerfulness. There may occasionally be tactlessness and unpredictability.

Saturn—independent and an original thinker with determination and ambition. There can be a tendency to change suddenly and an obstinate streak. Often good with scientific pursuits.

Uranus—friendly and caring, supporting good causes. Quite innovative and independent. Likely to be unpredictable.

Neptune—this placing will be found only from the last year or two of this century.

Pluto—it is unlikely that this placing will be found.

The Planets in Pisces

Moon—caring, sympathetic, very helpful and hospitable but tend to be vulnerable. This means that although they have a great deal to offer, they may find the real world a little harsh.

Mercury—intuitive, sympathetic, caring and with a desire to help others. However can be forgetful and lacking in confidence.

Venus—very emotional and sentimental. May be gullible and easily deceived. Relationships may flounder between the realities and the hopes, or fantasies.

Mars—imaginative and intuitive, but generally quite impractical even though creative. Gentle and artistic but lacks commitment.

Jupiter—sympathetic and understanding and able to get on well with others. Imaginative and yet needs targets to aim for. Can be self-indulgent or subject to self-deception.

Saturn—intuitive, idealistic and imaginative with a flair for creative outlets. However, such people tend to be shy and inhibited, and there is often a tendency to worry.

Uranus—idealistic, caring but especially with an originality and inventiveness that may be truly inspired. May follow the crowd, even into trouble, but generally this can be overcome.

Neptune—this will not be found.

Pluto—this will not be found.

Progressions and Transits

Progressions and transits are additional tools in the application and use of astrological charts. However they should be used only after the basic skills of chart construction and interpretation have been achieved. Progressions are used to construct a chart for someone who is now thirty-five, say, and the birth chart is modified accordingly. The progression used most is called the *Day-for-a-Year Progression* (or secondary direction). In this case a day is added for each year of the individual's life. Thus, for someone born on 3 January 1971, to work out progression for them aged twenty-one, 21 is added to the 3 to make 24. The planetary positions on 24 January 1971 are equivalent to the progressed planets for 1992 at the age of twenty-one. If, by adding the number of days (equivalent to years) to the birth day, the number goes beyond the month end then the number of days in the month is subtracted and a day in the following month is used. Thus, using the same example, someone aged thirty would progress the date to 3 + 30 = 33, which, less the thirty-one days of January, leaves 2 February as the progressed chart.

The planets are then plotted as before by reference to the ephemeris, and can be placed on the natal (birth) chart for comparison. The method of interpretation is essentially the same as for the natal chart with construction of aspects with their attendant meanings.

Transits are the movements of a planet through a sign or house and are read in relation to the birth chart. This can bring about significant changes if the planet changes house, sign or both. In addition, if the planet is in retrograde motion, it can pass backwards over a particular point. If a planet changes to retrograde motion, it can go back over a point and thereby the effect may be one of great change. Essentially, a retrograde planet, whatever its origin (natal, progression or transit), will bring stress.

All the planets move at different rates and therefore the transits will last for different times. The Moon transits quickly (a few hours), while Jupiter and Saturn may take up to a year, and the outermost planets (Uranus, Neptune and Pluto) up to eighteen months.

Applications of Astrology

When birth charts, progression and transits have been calculated and achieved with some degree of proficiency, the interpretations can be made to specific effect. There are many ways in which astrology can be used:

chart comparison—charts of two people can be compared to see whether they are compatible in their personalities and whether a relationship is likely to be successful. This study is also called synastry. This, in conjunction with the next category, can be used to study marriage prospects.

sexual matters—this has to be dealt with very carefully but may assist in determining likely success of a relationship on these grounds.

employment—the job, career, business moves, can all be analysed and it may be that strengths can be identified that will suit someone to a particular career.

Relationships

Relationships in general are an interesting part of astrology, and there are particular parts of a birth chart that indicate how people will interact in any sort of partnership. The planets have the same significance in this area of astrology as described elsewhere in the book, but the summary below relates specifically to relationships:

The *Moon* shows how you (assuming you are the subject) respond to your partner on a emotional level. Mercury, with its preponderance for communication, will focus on the interchange of ideas and thoughts. Venus represents love but also possessions, which are clearly important factors when considering relationships. Physical and sexual energy is represented by Mars, and the partner with the most powerful placing of this planet could well dominate a partnership. Expansion is the theme of Jupiter, and this can be interpreted to reflect how one partner opens up the relationship and how intellectually stimulating the partnership is likely to be. The control and limiting nature of Saturn can have a very important influence on the charts. Its influence will be enhanced if it makes a strong aspect to the Sun, or a personal planet. The remaining planets, Uranus, Neptune and Pluto, all move slowly and are very likely to occupy the same signs in both charts under consideration. Their importance should therefore not be overdone unless they form personal planets. Uranus represents change and can be a source of problems while Neptune brings elements of romance. Pluto is influential in matters where difficulties have to be resolved, but it can also prove to be a barrier to progress.

The comparison of charts has to be done very carefully, and the information about the planets can either be placed on the one chart, or the second set of angular placings can be plotted around the edge of the first chart. A list of planets should be made for clarity and a grid depicting all the aspects. When this is done, a start can be made on identifying the significance of respective aspects and their interpretation.

Business and careers

Another area in which there is considerable interest is that of business and the career. Of course no one ca-

reer is associated with any particular sign of chart,
but there are some basic guidelines. In guiding someone to a certain career, based upon their chart, a
number of features should be considered carefully.
The ascendant will indicate their willingness to work
hard and how enthusiastic they will be, while the
midheaven indicates their hopes. The changeable aspect of the Moon shows how the subject will react to
changes in the workplace, respond to customers and
whether they will prefer a quiet or hectic work environment. Some of the houses have particular influence. If a personal planet occurs in the twelfth house,
then a quiet solitary occupation may suit best. Conversely, the first house would probably suggest a job
where there is a lot of contact with people and where
the pace is quite hectic. Placings of the planets may
also suggest a particular skill, and these aspects
should also be taken into account. One or more careers will begin to show themselves in the chart
through the presence of creative ability, practical or
scientific ability, the talent for organizing or a leaning
towards the health and caring professions. A complete picture can be built up using all the available
information, which ultimately leads to a small
number of possible careers becoming apparent.

The Sun signs do lead to certain suggestions for
careers, for example, depending upon the placing of

the ascendant, those with the Sun sign Aries might consider the armed forces, self-employment, the media, charity work, sports or academia.

Sport and leisure

A similar procedure can be used to determine the likely sporting and leisure activities for someone. Additional factors would be taken into account, however, such as general health and physical make-up, age and the nature of the leisure, i.e. is a repetitive sport required to allow for a time of mental reflection and perhaps to compensate for a challenging job, or, conversely, is a demanding, highly active pastime necessary to create the excitement missing in everyday employment. As in the case of the career, the Sun sign will suggest some possibilities, depending on the placing of the ascendant. Thus the Sun sign Arian may opt for DIY, writing, dancing or music in the creative vein or jogging, canoeing tennis or athletics for physical activity.

Other aspects of life can also be studied, such as health and psychological facets, and the planets, their house positions and transits all have significance.